Anonymous

Correspondence Relating to the Non-Fulfilment

by the Dominion of Canada of that part of the terms of Confederation which guarantees efficient steam service for the conveyance of mails and passengers between Prince Edward Island and the mainland

Anonymous

Correspondence Relating to the Non-Fulfilment
by the Dominion of Canada of that part of the terms of Confederation which guarantees efficient steam service for the conveyance of mails and passengers between Prince Edward Island and the mainland

ISBN/EAN: 9783337175405

Printed in Europe, USA, Canada, Australia, Japan

Cover: Foto ©ninafisch / pixelio.de

More available books at **www.hansebooks.com**

CORRESPONDENCE

Relating to the Non-fulfilment by the Dominion of Canada of that part of the Terms of Confederation which guarantees Efficient Steam Service for the Conveyance of Mails and Passengers between Prince Edward Island and the Mainland.

To His Excellency, the Right Honorable Sir John Douglas Cutherland Campbell (commonly called the Marquis of Lorne), Knight of the Most Ancient and Most Noble Order of the Thistle, Knight Grand Cross of the Most Distinguished Order of St. Michael and St. George, Governor General of Canada, and Vice Admiral of the same, &c., &c., &c.

We, Her Majesty's dutiful and loyal subjects, the Legislative Council and House of Assembly of Prince Edward Island, in General Assembly convened, approach Your Excellency, and represent:

1. That upon the first day of July, 1873, Prince Edward Island entered the Confederation of the Dominion of Canada, upon certain terms and conditions set forth in an Order of Her Majesty the Queen, in Council, dated 26th June, 1873.

2. That in the said terms and conditions of Union, it was expressly stipulated that the Dominion Government should assume and defray all the charges for the establishment and maintenance of efficient Steam Service for the conveyance of Mails and Passengers between this Island and the Mainland of the Dominion, winter and summer, so as to place this Island in continuous communication with the Intercolonial Railway and the Railway system of the Dominion.

3. That during no winter season intervening between the year 1873 and the present time, has the Steam Service provided by the Dominion Government been efficient, or the communication with the Mainland in any degree continuous.

4. That during the first winter season after the Union, no attempt was made by the General Government to provide such Steam Service; that during the two subsequent winter seasons, viz: those of 1874-5, and 1875-6, a wooden steamboat, called the *Albert*, was placed upon the route between Georgetown and Pictou, but she failed to perform the service satisfactorily. That at the commencement of the winter season

of 1876–7 a new steamer called the *Northern Light*, which had been constructed expressly for the work, was placed upon the route.

5. That the records of the trips made by this Steamboat are inaccessible to us, but it is notorious that these trips have been most irregular and unsatisfactory, and that at times she has been detained, ice-bound, for periods ranging from ten to twenty-four days, to the imminent danger of the Passengers and Mails. On more than one occasion during the present winter, some of the Passengers, among whom were several females and children, were forced, after remaining on board the vessel for several days, to leave her and walk a distance of many miles to the shore, when night overtaking them, they received severe injuries from cold and exposure, and one of them has been crippled for life.

6. That the people of this Province have suffered great loss by reason of the frequent interruption to the winter Steam Service, involving extraordinary delay, not only in the transmission of important letters by mail, but also in the conveyance of Passengers, thereby causing serious derangement to trade and immense inconvenience to the entire community.

7. That the experience of the last five years fully convinces us that the Steamer *Northern Light* is totally unfitted to perform that efficient service undertaken by the Dominion Government, and as we are of opinion that ample time has been allowed for experiments, we submit that means should be adopted without further delay, to secure to this Province continuous communication, in accordance with the terms of Union.

8. That one of the principal inducements held out to this Province to enter the Confederation, was the promise of constant communication with the Mainland, and the prospect of participating in the benefits arising from the Intercolonial Railway, and other Public Works, from which its inhabitants had been previously debarred for a large portion of the year, and to the maintenance of which they are called upon to contribute, without deriving any corresponding advantage.

9. We submit that the good faith of the Dominion Government is pledged to the fulfilment of the compact of Confederation, involving the establishment and maintenance of efficient Steam Service with the Mainland, and continuous communication with the Intercolonial and other Dominion Railways, and we represent that Prince Edward Island is justly entitled to receive from the Dominion, compensation for the non-fulfilment by the Dominion Government of the terms of Union in the particular herein mentioned.

Wherefore the Legislative Council and House of Assembly pray that Your Excellency in Council will take the foregoing facts into your most serious consideration, and adopt vigorous and immediate measures to remedy the grievance complained of, and cause to be placed at the disposal of Prince Edward Island, the compensation to which the Province is entitled, by reason of the non-fulfilment by the Dominion of the terms of Confederation.

And as in duty bound we will ever pray.

Certified,

JOHN BALL, C. L. C.
FREDERICK W. HUGHES, A. C. H. A.

No. 18.

PROVINCE OF PRINCE EDWARD ISLAND,

Government House, 7th April, 1881.

SIR :—

I have the honor to transmit herewith a Joint Address from the Legislative Council and House of Assembly to His Excellency the Governor General, praying that immediate measures may be adopted by the Dominion Government to fulfil the Terms of Confederation with Prince Edward Island by establishing and maintaining efficient Steam Service for the convoyance of Mails and Passengers between the Island and the Mainland of the Dominion, Winter and Summer, thus placing the Province in continuous communication with the Intercolonial Railway and the Railway system of the Dominion, and by causing to be placed at the disposal of the Island compensation for the failure on the part of the Dominion to carry out said terms; and also a Joint Address from the Council and Assembly requesting me to cause the said Address to His Excellency to be laid before him.

I have the honor to be,

Sir,

Your obedient servant,

T. HEATH HAVILAND,

Lieutenant Governor.

The Honorable

The Secretary of State, Ottawa.

838
on
7/5.

OTTAWA, 16th April, 1881.

:—

I am directed to acknowledge the receipt of your despatch of the 7th instant, en ng a Joint Address of the Legislative Council and House of Assembly of the Province of Prince Edward Island, in reference to the establishment and maintenance of Steam service for the conveyance of Mails and Passengers between that Province and the Mainland.

I have the honor to be,

Sir,

Your obedient servant,

EDOUARD J. LANGEVIN,

Under Secretary of State.

His Honor

The Lieutenant Governor of

Prince Edward Island, Charlottetown.

No. 9.

PROVINCE OF PRINCE EDWARD ISLAND,

Government House, 28th February, 1882.

SIR:—

My Government having, by a Minute of Council, recommended me to bring to the notice of the Dominion Government that this Province is yet without a reply from the Privy Council of Canada to the Joint Address of the Legislative Council and House of Assembly, passed last Session, on the subject of the failure of the Dominion Government to carry out the terms of Confederation by providing continuous communication, winter and summer, between this Island and the Mainland Provinces of the Dominion.

As the General Assembly meets on the 7th of March, my Government are anxious to have the reply with as little delay as possible.

I have the honor to be,

Sir,

Your obedient Servant,

T. HEATH HAVILAND

Lieutenant Governor.

The Honorable

The Secretary of State, Ottawa.

421
on
1227.

OTTAWA, 8th March. 1882.

SIR:—

I have the honor to acknowledge the receipt of your Despatch, No. 9, of the 28th ult., requesting a reply to the Joint Address of the Legislative Council and House of

Assembly of the Province of Prince Edward Island, passed during their last Session, respecting continuous communication between that Province and the Mainland Provinces of the Dominion.

I have the honor to be,
Sir,
Your obedient servant,
EDOUARD J. LANGEVIN,
Under Secretary of State.

His Honor
The Lieutenant Governor of
Prince Edward Island, Charlottetown.

Extract from Minutes of Executive Council of Prince Edward Island.

COUNCIL CHAMBER,

January 31st, 1883.

At a meeting of the Executive Council in Committee.

PRESENT:

The Honorables Messieurs

SULLIVAN, FERGUSON,
CAMPBELL, PROWSE,
MACLEOD, LEFURGEY,
ARSENAULT.

The Executive Council in Committee have had under consideration the failure of the Dominion Government to fulfil that condition of the Terms of Confederation, which stipulates that the Government of Canada shall assume "and defray all the charges for the establishment and maintenance of efficient Steam Service for the conveyance of Mails and Passengers, between Prince Edward Island and the Mainland of the Dominion, winter and summer, so as to place the Island in continuous communication with the Intercolonial Railway, and the Railway system of the Dominion."

In a Joint Address of the Legislative Council and House of Assembly of this Province, to His excellency the Governor General, adopted in the Session of 1881, were set forth the enormous disadvantages under which the inhabitants of this Island labor, by reason of the insufficiency of the means provided for the transport of mails and passengers, during the winter season, and a request was made for the immediate adoption of vigorous measures for the removal of the grievances complained of, as well as for the allowance of compensation by reason of the non-fulfilment, in such respect, of the Terms of Confederation. The receipt of this Address was duly acknowledged by the Secretary of State, in a Despatch dated 16th April, 1881, and upon the notice of the Dominion Government being again directed thereto, and a reply requested, it was learned that the question was receiving their earnest consideration.

The Council in Committee desire to draw the attention of the General Government to the fact that, although nearly two years have elapsed since the acknowledgment of the receipt of the said Address, no attempt has been made to improve the means of communication with the Mainland Provinces of the Dominion, and that the grievances complained of therein still remain.

During the first winter succeeding the Union, it was not expected that much could be effected towards providing "continuous communication," but the inhabitants of the Island patiently awaited the result of the experiment being made, by the Dominion Government, to demonstrate the practicability of the winter navigation of the Gulf of St. Lawrence. The futile attempts of the steamer *Northern Light*, during the last seven years, to maintain "continuous communication" are notorious. Experience warrants the assertion that she is unfitted for the service; her trips, during the few weeks of winter in which she runs, are irregular and unsatisfactory; her carrying capacity is exceedingly limited, and her model is generally condemned.

A strong inducement for this Province to enter the Confederation was the promise of "continuous communication with the Intercolonial Railway and the Railway system of the Dominion."—A service that would be as thoroughly efficient and regular as the Railways with which such communication was guaranteed:—in short, that Prince Edward Island should have equal facilities for intercourse with the other Provinces, as those Provinces enjoy between themselves, and should participate in all the benefits arising from the Intercolonial Railway, and other Public Works upon the Mainland, from which it had formerly been debarred for a great portion of the year, and to which it contributes without receiving any corresponding advantage.

The inconvenience and loss sustained by the people of this Province, in consequence of the imperfect means of winter transport, are incalculable. Irregularity of the mail se[illegible]ce, in which delays of ten consecutive days are often experienced,—the consequent derangement of business,—the hardships of travelling, which only the strong and robust are able to endure;—the dangers attendant upon the winter routes; —the total stoppage of all transport for freight or merchandize;—these are some of the disadvantages attending the present mode of winter communication between this Province and the Mainland.

Of continuous steam communication, summer and winter, with the Mainland, Prince Edward Island received an assurance and guarantee at the time of its entry into the Confederation in 1873. Nearly ten years have now elapsed since that event, and but one abortive attempt has been made by the General Government to carry out the solemn engagement into which they then entered. It is not the office of the Government of this Province to dictate to the Dominion Government as to the way in which they shall carry out the Terms of Union, in respect to "continuous communication," but the Council in Committee are bound to express the opinion that only a very feeble attempt has been made to accomplish this object, and that the means of attaining this most desirable end have not been nearly exhausted.

To carry out the Terms of Confederation with British Columbia, the Dominion is expending an immense sum of money in the construction of the Pacific Railway, yet to provide the means of communication between two Provinces, over a distance of scarcely nine miles, and thus fulfil an obligation equally as binding as that with British Columbia, the General Government have displayed a marked indifference.

The Council in Committee feel that the Government of Canada are justly chargeable with a most serious violation of the Terms of Union in this respect; they desire, once more, to bring the matter prominently before the notice of Your Excellency in Council, with the earnest hope that the ensuing session of Parliament will not be allowed to pass without the adoption of effective measures for the immediate fulfilment of the Terms of Confederation; they request that they may be furnished with a reply to the Address of the Council and Assembly herein referred to, as well as to this Minute, in sufficient time to submit the same to the Legislature of this Province, at the approaching Session thereof. Should the Dominion Government fail to comply with the just request of this Province, its Government will be reluctantly compelled to lay the grievances complained of at the foot of the Throne, and to appeal for redress to Her Majesty the Queen, as one of the parties to the Articles of Confederation.

Certified, a true Extract,

R. F. DE BLOIS,
Clerk Executive Council.

[COPY.]

MEMORANDUM.

Referring to a Minute of the Executive Council of Prince Edward Island, dated 31st January last, to the Address of the Legislative Council and House of Assembly therein mentioned, and to interviews with the Privy Council of Canada on the subject of efficient Steam Communication between the Island and the Mainland, in accordance with the Terms of Confederation, the undersigned desire to request that the Government of Prince Edward Island be placed in possession of the reply of the Dominion Government in such form as they can submit to the Provincial Legislature, which will meet on the 20th March, instant.

(Signed) W. W. SULLIVAN,
DONALD FERGUSON,
SAMUEL PROWSE.

Ottawa, March 3rd, 1883.

[TELEGRAMS.]

CHARLOTTETOWN, 27th March, 1883.

To the Secretary of State, Ottawa:

Required immediately to lay before the Legislature now in Session, Dominion Government's answer to joint Address of Legislature of April, 1881, relative to Steam Communication with Mainland, and also to Minute of Council of January last upon the same subject.

T. HEATH HAVILAND

Lieutenant Governor.

OTTAWA, 28th March, 1883.

To the Lieutenant Governor:

Subject referred to in your Message of twenty-seventh instant under consideration.

G. POWELL,

Under-Secretary of State.

To His Excellency the Most Honorable Sir HENRY CHARLES KEITH PETTY FITZMAURICE, Marquis of Lansdowne, Governor General of Canada, and Vice Admiral of the same, &c., &c., &c., in Council.

Her Majesty's dutiful and loyal subjects, the Legislative Council and House of Assembly of Prince Edward Island, in General Assembly convened, approach Your Excellency, and represent that,—

During the Session of 1881 they addressed the Governor General of Canada in Council, calling attention to the fact that the General Government had failed to carry out one of the conditions of the compact under which Prince Edward Island entered the Confederation of the Dominion of Canada, viz:—

"To establish and maintain efficient Steam Service for the conveyance of Mails and Passengers between the Island and the Dominion, Winter and Summer, thus placing the Island in continuous communication with the Intercolonial Railway and the Railway system of the Dominion."

At the same time they prayed for the adoption of vigorous and immediate measures for remedying the grievances complained of, as well as for compensation to this Province on account of the non-fulfilment by the Dominion of the terms of Confederation.

The receipt of this Address was duly acknowledged by the Secretary of State in a Despatch dated 16th April, 1881, and upon the notice of the Dominion Government being again called thereto, assurances were returned in both of the years 1882 and 1883, that the question was under their consideration.

Notwithstanding that three Sessions of the Dominion Parliament have been held since the receipt of their Address aforementioned, no improvement whatever has been made in the means of winter communication, and the Legislature of this Province are not aware that as a result of the investigation of the question during the three years which have elapsed, the General Government have decided upon any definite steps towards an absolute fulfilment of their obligations.

In this, the eleventh year of their connection with the Dominion of Canada, instead of enjoying that efficient and continuous Steam communication with the Mainland, guaranteed them at the time of their entry into the Confederation, for a very considerable portion of the year the people of Prince Edward Island are entirely dependent upon a mode that was in use before steam power was applied to the propulsion of vessels.

During all this time they have patiently awaited the fulfilment, by the General Government, of the terms of Confederation in this particular respect, until the Legislature are reluctantly constrained to say that, in their opinion, the Dominion Government have evinced a marked indifference, not only for the welfare of Prince Edward Island, but for the inviolability of their own obligations as well.

During the first winter succeeding the Union, the people of this Province did not expect that much could possibly be effected towards providing "continuous communication," neither was anything attempted in such respect; but they anticipated, at the least, that the matter would receive the early and earnest consideration of the Government, who would be only too anxious to carry out the pledged faith of the Dominion to the smallest and most helpless of its Provinces. Not so, however; but for the three consecutive winters the fulfilment of their guarantee was mocked by the employment of an old vessel called the *Albert*, whose usefulness in every other sphere of navigation had long previously departed.

Eventually, in 1877, a steamer, the *Northern Light*, which had been built for service in the St. Lawrence River, near Quebec, was purchased by the Government, and placed on the route between Georgetown and Pictou, where she has continued up to the present time.

Whatever may be the general opinion of the work performed by the *Northern Light* during the last seven years, of this fact there is no doubt: that for an average of eight weeks in each winter she is laid up; that during the time she runs her trips are uncertain, irregular, and unsatisfactory, and the accommodation afforded is neither continuous nor efficient. While the *Northern Light* has, no doubt, been useful in demonstrating the practicability of the winter navigation of the Straits of Northumberland, the Legislature submit that she has proved herself utterly incapable of successfully overcoming its difficulties; and they observe, with regret, that the only

3

improvement contemplated is the adaptation in some way of a steamer intended for the Lighthouse service, so as to supplement the work of the *Northern Light*.

The Legislature consider it almost unnecessary to recount the peculiar disadvantages under which this Province labors, owing to its insular position, for they feel that, from the constant representations which have been made, the Government and Parliament of Canada cannot be ignorant of them, and it is for this reason that the people of the Island are inclined to the belief that they are the victims of a serious injustice at the hands of a body who should protect their interests.

Cut off, as they always were, for nearly five months of the year from all communication with the Mainland, except by a most uncertain and dangerous route, a promise of continuous communication with the Intercolonial Railway and the Railways of the Dominion was indeed a strong inducement to them to surrender their self-government and unite with Canada. They naturally expected that, within a reasonable time, they would possess uninterrupted communication, at all seasons of the year, with the rest of Canada and of the world—that they would enjoy equal facilities for intercourse with the other Provinces as those Provinces enjoy between themselves, and would participate in all the benefits arising from the Intercolonial Railway and other public works upon the Mainland, from which they had previously been debarred for a great portion of the year.

The inconvenience and loss which they have suffered in consequence of the failure of the Federal Government to provide them with the efficient communication promised are incalculable, while the disappointment to their expectations has not tended to enhance, in their estimation, the value of a connection with the Dominion, but on the contrary, has awakened a feeling of discontent which, though a matter of regret, is not unnatural under the circumstances.

Were it only the transport of freight and merchandize that was stopped during the winter season, they would have good reason to complain of being precluded from the benefits of the Intercolonial and other Railways which their more fortunate neighbors on the Mainland enjoy; but their complaint, as well, is that in direct violation of the compact upon which they entered the Confederation, no efficient and continuous means of Steam Communication have been provided whereby Mails and Passengers can be transported to the Mainland. The derangement of business consequent upon the irregularity of the Mail service, when, for ten days at times, no communication whatever is had with the rest of Canada, exercises a most prejudicial effect upon their interests. The hardships of travelling, which only the strong and robust are able to endure, and the dangers attendant upon the present mode, are other disadvantages from which they suffer most acutely.

The feeling that they are being unjustly treated is not without great foundation. As members of one vast country, the welfare of all is assuredly the object to be attained, and where difficulties or hardships militate against the prosperity of the people, their removal is undertaken by the General Government. On what other ground can the vast system of Railways, Canals and other public works be accounted for than as means to overcome distance and to remove difficulties of transport? So rapidly has Canada grown since Confederation, that the means of communication are found not to keep pace with the rate at which the country is developing, and millions of dollars are being annually spent in linking together the scattered Provinces from the Atlantic to the Pacific. But three years ago the Federal Parliament, in order to keep faith with British Columbia, a Province of little more than ten thousand of a population, contracted for the construction of over two thousand miles of railway at a cost of millions of dollars; yet the fulfilment of the Terms of Union with Prince Edward Island, a Province of equal importance at least with British Columbia, by providing the means of communication over a Strait less than nine miles wide, is postponed from year to year without any thought, as it would seem, that thereby a solemn and binding obligation is being broken, and an immense injury being done to its people.

The Legislature of Prince Edward Island are satisfied that this state of things cannot longer continue without a breach of that harmony which is so indispensable between the Provinces of the Confederation. They feel that the Province is being treated invidiously and unjustly, and that its prosperity is retarded, in a great degree, by the failure to afford that efficient communication with the rest of the world so necessary to an agricultural community.

Were the General Government asked, as a matter of grace, to grant continuous communication with the Mainland, some reasonable ground might exist for refusing to do so; but when the request is only that they fulfil their obligations, and carry out their pledged faith, by providing efficient Steam service, Summer and Winter, their neglect to do so is inexcusable.

The Legislature of Prince Edward Island are of opinion that the Government of Canada are justly chargeable with a most serious violation of the Terms of Union in the manner which they have pointed out, and they desire to bring again the matter prominently before the notice of Your Excellency in Council, in order to the adoption of immediate and effective measures for the absolute fulfilment of the Terms of Confederation, or otherwise that they may be informed that Your Excellency's Government are either unable or unwilling to abide by their compact.

The Legislature submit that on every principle of justice this Province should receive compensation in view of the immense loss and disadvantage which have accrued by reason of the failure of the General Government to provide the efficient and continuous communication guaranteed by the Terms of Confederation, and they therefore claim, as due to the present time, the sum of $5,000,000, to which they consider this Province justly entitled.

The Legislature trust that this most important matter, which they now, for the last time, bring under the notice of the General Government, may immediately engage their attention, and that a favorable answer will be accorded without delay, otherwise the Legislature desire that the Government of the Province invoke the interference of Her Majesty the Queen, by laying a statement of the grievances complained of at the foot of the Throne.

Certified,

JOHN BALL, C. L. C.
FREDERICK W. HUGHES, A. C. H. A.

No. 8.

GOVERNMENT HOUSE,
Charlottetown, P. E. Island,
18th April, 1884.

SIR:—

I have the honor to transmit herewith, to be laid before His Excellency the Governor General, a Joint Address from the Legislative Council and House of Assembly to His Excellency the Governor General representing the failure of the Dominion Government to carry out that part of the terms of Confederation which requires the Government of Canada to "establish and maintain efficient steam service for the conveyance of mails and passengers between the Island and the Mainland of the Dominion, winter and summer, thus placing the Island in continuous communication with the Intercolonial Railway, and the Railway system of the Dominion;" and praying that His Excellency in Council will take such action as shall cause the grievance complained of to be remedied, and the Terms of Union to be fulfilled, as well as praying that compensation be paid to Prince Edward Island for the nonfulfilment of said terms.

I have the honor to be,

Sir,

Your obedient servant,

T. HEATH HAVILAND,
Lieutenant Governor.

The Honorable
The Secretary of State, Ottawa.

770
on
2912.

OTTAWA, 24th April, 1884.

SIR:—

I have the honor to acknowledge the receipt of your Despatch No. 8, of the 18th instant, transmitting, in order that the said may be laid before His Excellency the Governor General, a Joint Address from the Legislative Council and House of Assembly of Prince Edward Island, on the subject of an efficient steam service for the conveyance of mails and passengers between that Province and the Mainland of the Dominion, winter and summer, and to state that this matter will receive due consideration.

I have the honor to be,

Sir,

Your obedient servant,

G. POWELL,

Under Secretary of State.

His Honor

The Lieutenant Governor of

Prince Edward Island, Charlottetown.

Extract from Minutes of Executive Council of Prince Edward Island.

COUNCIL CHAMBER,

February 20th, 1885.

At a meeting of the Executive Council in Committee.

The following Minute was adopted and ordered to be handed to His Honor the Lieutenant Governor for transmission to the Dominion Government:

Adverting to the Joint Address of the Legislative Council and House of Assembly, in the Session of 1884, to His Excellency the Governor General in Council (a copy of which is herewtth transmitted) upon the subject of the nonfulfilment of the Terms of Confederation, in respect to Communication with the Mainland, the Executive Council in Committee desire to bring to the notice of His Excellency in Council in fact that, beyond a formal acknowledgment of the receipt of the said Address, no reply thereto has been received.

Without entering into a recapitulation of the statements set forth in the said Address, the Council in Committee wish to draw His Excellency's attention to the several steps which have been taken by this Province towards securing the fulfilment ot the Compact of Confederation in the particular alluded to, and which have proved so far entirely unsuccessful. And here they desire to express their surprise and regret at the extraordinary apathy with which the interests of Prince Edward Island have been treated in this regard.

Trusting implicitly in the good faith of the General Government, the people of this Province waited patiently, for seven years, the fulfilment of the Terms of Confederation, until in 1881, the Legislative Council and House of Assembly united in an Address to His Excellency the Governor General, setting forth the disadvantages under which they labored, praying for the adoption of vigorous and immediate measures to remedy the grievances complained of, and requesting compensation for loss sustained by reason of the delay which had occurred.

The receipt of this Address was formally acknowledged on 16th April, 1881, but no other reply was received. On 28th February, 1882, the Lieutenant Governor of this Province communicated with the Secretary of State, directing attention to the Address, and to the fact that it had not been answered, when subsequently a reply was received that the Government of Canada were giving their earnest consideration to the question.

Another year having passed, the Council in Committee, on the 31st January, 1883, drew the attention of the General Government to the fact that, although nearly two years had elapsed since the receipt of the Address of 1881, no attempt had been made to improve the means of Communication, and that the grievances complained of in the said Address still remained. Upon 3rd March following, the Provincial Government requested a reply to the Minute of 31st January, in such form as could be submitted to the Legislature then about to meet. No answer being received, on 27th March the Lieutenant Governor telegraphed to the Secretary of State, and was informed in reply that the subject was under consideration.

Wearied with long waiting and ineffectual applications, the Legislative Council and House of Assembly, at their last Session, again approached His Excellency in Council, renewing the relation of their grievances, but, as already mentioned, beyond a simple acknowledgment, their appeal has been unsuccessful.

Why the claim of Prince Edward Island to a fulfilment of the Compact by which Canada secured its adhesion to the Confederation, should be so persistently ignored, it is difficult to conceive. By a contract entered into with extraordinary solemnity, the General Government agreed for certain considerations, to "establish and maintain efficient steam service for the conveyance of mails and passengers between the Island and the Mainland of the Dominion, winter and summer, thus placing the Island in continuous communication with the Intercolonial Railway and the railway system of the Dominion," yet during no year of nearly twelve which have elapsed since the Union, has the communication provided been such as was guaranteed. For eight or nine weeks each winter, the people of this Province are dependent, for their postal communication, upon a system in use among them long years before steam power was ever applied for purposes of locomotion. Unsatisfactory as this state of affairs is, it is aggravated by the neglect, during this period, to provide any means whatever for the transport of passengers, and it is only as a matter of favor on the part of the Mail Couriers that persons are enabled to make the passage, and then only in open boats, which are wholly unprovided with the means of sustenance, warmth or shelter, and at the imminent peril of their lives. To shew that this language is not extravagant, it is only necessary to refer to the experience of the crew and passengers, twenty-two in number, who, in January last, were detained on the ice between Capes Traverse and Tormentine for two days and one night, during which they suffered most severely, and from which many of them will never entirely recover.

The Address of last Session imposed upon the Provincial Government the duty, in the event of a favorable answer not being accorded thereto without delay, of invoking the interference of Her Majesty the Queen to obtain that justice which the Island has been so long denied. While it is a subject of deep regret that the Dominion Government have not seen fit to take any action in the matter therein pressed upon their notice, the Council in Committee feel that no alternative is left to them than to lay at the foot of the Throne a statement of the grievances so long endured, and ask of Her Majesty, as one of the contracting parties to the Articles of Confederation that she will be graciously pleased to secure to Prince Edward Island that redress which has so repeatedly been sought, but which has not yet been obtained.

Certified, a true Extract,

R. F. DE BLOIS,

Clerk Executive Council.

GOVERNMENT HOUSE,

Charlottetown, Prince Edward Island,

February, 28th, 1885.

SIR :—

I have the honor to transmit herewith for the consideration of His Excellency the Governor General in Council, an approved minute of my Council, passed on the 30th inst., upon the subject of the non-fulfilment of the Terms of Confederation in respect to Communication with the Mainland, together with the copy therein referred to of the Address of the Legislature of the Island, as passed in the Session of 1884, on the same subject.

I have the honor to be,

Sir,

Your obedient Servant,

(Signed) A. A. MACDONALD,

Lieutenant Governor.

The Honorable

The Secretary of State, Ottawa.

788
on
3993

OTTAWA, 6th March, 1885.

SIR:—

I have the honor to acknowledge the receipt of your despatch of the 28th ultimo, transmitting for submission to His Excellency the Governor General an approved Minute of the Executive Council of Prince Edward Island, in respect to Winter Communication with the Mainland, together with a copy to which the same refers of the Address of the Legislature of the Island, as passed in the season of 1884, upon the subject, and to state that the same will receive due consideration.

I have the honor to be,

Sir,

Your obedient servant,

(Signed) G. POWELL,

Under Secretary of State.

His Honor

The Lieutenant Governor of

Prince Edward Island, Charlottetown.

To His Honor the Honorable ANDREW ARCHIBALD MACDONALD, Lieutenant Governor of the Province of Prince Edward Island, &c., &c., &c.

MAY IT PLEASE YOUR HONOR,—

Whereas, During the present Session of the General Assembly, the House of Assembly did join with the Legislative Council in a memorial to Her Majesty the Queen, praying Her Majesty's most gracious intervention in order to obtain from the Government of Canada a fulfilment of the terms upon which this Island entered the Confederation, in respect to Communication with the Mainland, and also the payment of compensation to this Province for the loss sustained by its people in consequence of the failure of the Dominion Government to carry out the said terms; and a Joint Address of both Houses has been adopted requesting His Honor the Lieutenant Governor to forward the said memorial to His Excellency the Governor General, for transmission to Her Majesty the Queen.

And Whereas, Since the adoption of the said memorial and Address, an insurrection has unfortunately been incited in the Northwest Territories, whereby not only the peace and wellfare of the Dominion have been disturbed, but the lives and property of its citizens are endangered, while some of Her Majesty's subjects have met their death in bravely endeavoring to uphold the Authority of the British Crown.

And Whereas, This House recognizes the paramount obligation of the Genera

Government to suppress lawlessness and rebellion, and it is the imperative duty of every British subject to assist the constituted authorities in the restoration of quietness and good order, and in the maintenance of the Queen's supremacy.

Therefore this House, unwilling to embarrass the General Government while occupied with matters of such weighty moment to the Empire and looking to a speedy termination of the insurrection, desire to postpone for the present the carrying out of the constitutional means by which it seeks to redress a grievance of the people of this Province, and request your Honor not to forward the said memorial until such time during the approaching Legislative recess, as in the opinion of your advisers shall be deemed opportune.

Certified,

FREDERICK W. HUGHES, A. C. H. A.

To His Honor the Honorable ANDREW ARCHIBALD MACDONALD, Lieutenant Governor of the Province of Prince Edward Island, &c., &c., &c.

MAY IT PLEASE YOUR HONOR,—

Whereas, During the present Session of the General Assembly, this House did join with the House of Assembly in a memorial to Her Majesty the Queen praying Her Majesty's most gracious intervention in order to obtain from the Government of Canada a fulfilment of the the terms upon which this Island entered the Confederation, in respect to Communication with the Mainland, and also the payment of compensation to this Province for the loss sustained by its people in consequence of the failure of the Dominion Government to carry out the said terms; and a Joint Address of both Houses has been adopted requesting your Honor to forward the said memorial to His Excellency the Governor General, for transmission to Her Majesty the Queen.

And Whereas, Since the adoption of the said memorial and Address, an insurrection has unfortunately been incited in the Northwest Provinces, whereby not only the peace and wellfare of the Dominion have been disturbed, but the lives and property of its citizens are endangered, while some of Her Mrjesty's subjects have met their death in bravely endeavoring to uphold the authority of the British Crown.

And Whereas, This House recognizes the paramount obligation of the General Government to suppress lawlessness and rebellion, and it is the imperative duty of every British subject to assist the constituted authorities in the restoration of quietness and good order, and in the maintenance of the Queen's supremacy.

Therefore this House, unwilling to embarrass the General Government while occupied with matters of such weighty moment to the Empire and looking to a speedy termination of the insurrection, desire to postpone for the present the carrying out of the constitutional means by which it seeks to redress a grievance of the people of this

Province, and request your Honor not to forward the said memorial until such time during the approaching Legislative recess, as in opinion of his advisers shall be deemed opportune.

Whilst this House regrets that an insurrection has been incited in the Northwest Territories, whereby not only the peace and welfare of the Dominion has been disturbed, but that the lives and property of its citizens have been endangered, yet as our case is a very urgent one in our opinion, there should be no unnecessary delay in forwarding the said memorial to Her Most Gracious Majesty the Queen, praying Her Majesty's most gracious intervention in order to obtain from the Government of Canada, a fulfilment of the Terms of Confederation in respect to Communication with the Mainland and also compensation to the Province for the loss sustained by its people in consequence of the failure of the Dominion Government to carry out said terms.

Certified,

JOHN BALL, C. L. C.

To the Queen's Most Excellent Majesty:

Most Gracious Sovereign,—We, your Majesty's most dutiful and loyal subjects, the Legislative Council and House of Assembly of Prince Edward Island, in General Assembly convened, humbly approach your Majesty and represent that:

1. Prince Edward Island entered the Confederation of the Dominion of Canada upon 1st July, 1873, on certain terms and conditions set forth in the order of Your Majesty in Council, dated 26th June, 1873, and of which terms the following is one: "The Dominion Government shall assume and defray all the charges for the following service, viz: Efficient Steam Service for the conveyance of Mails and Passengers, to be established and maintained between the Island and the Mainland of the Dominion, winter and summer, thus placing the Island in continuous communication with the Intercolonial Railway and the Railway system of the Dominion.

2. During no winter season since the time of the said Union has the service provided by the Dominion Government been efficient, or the communication with the Mainland continuous.

3. The Dominion Government having shown no sufficient disposition to fulfil their obligation towards the Island in this matter, we are reluctantly compelled to approach Your Majesty, as one of the parties to the articles of Confederation, and pray your Majesty's intervention to obtain for us that justice to which, as a Province of Canada, we are entitled by the Terms of Union.

4. Prince Edward Island is separated from the Mainland Provinces of Canada by

the Strait of Northumberland, and during the winter season, which generally begins about the first of December and lasts until the end of April, the harbors and rivers are frozen, while the passage of the Strait is impeded, though at no time wholly prevented by floating ice. Previous to the Union the only connection with the Mainland during winter was by means of ordinary boats, dragged across the drifting ice, and propelled by oars through the stretches of open water between Cape Traverse on the Island, and Cape Tormentine in New Brunswick—a distance of nine miles.

5. During the first winter after Confederation (1873–4) no attempt was made by the Dominion Government to provide such steam service. During the two subsequent years (1874-5, 1875-6) an old wooden steamboat, which had for years been engaged in ordinary navigation, but without a single qualification to fit her for the winter navigation of the Strait, was placed upon the route between Georgetown, one of the Island ports, and Pictou, in the Province of Nova Scotia; and, as was to be expected, she utterly failed in the service required of her. At the commencement of the winter 1876-7, a new steamer called the *Northern Light* was placed upon this route. This steamer was not constructed for the service, but was designed for another purpose, and therefore her work can be regarded only in the light of an experiment.

6. The service performed by the *Northern Light* has been most unsatisfactory, her trips being irregular, and the accommodation she afforded has been neither continuous nor efficient. According to the official returns for the last four years, there has been an average in each winter of sixty-four days, during which she has been entirely laid up. Nor does this furnish any idea of the irregularity of her trips before she entirely ceased running in each of these years, but only of the continued period when she was laid up and inoperative. At times she has been ice-bound for periods ranging from ten to twenty-four days, to the imminent danger of passengers and mails. Upon one occasion, four years ago, some of the passengers—among them women and children—were forced after remaining on board several days, to leave her and walk a distance of many miles to the shore, when night overtaking them, they received injuries from cold and exposure, which resulted ultimately in the death of one of the party.

7. During the time when the *Northern Light* is laid up, the people of the Island are obliged to resort to the old method of crossing between the Capes (Traverse and Tormentine) already described, a route attended with much hardship and great danger. In the month of January last a party of twenty-two persons were detained on the ice for two days and one night, in an attempt to make the passage, when they suffered most severely from cold and exposure—the majority of them being badly frozen—and several have since suffered amputation of their limbs as a result of the injuries then received.

8. One · the principal inducements held out to the people of this Island to

enter the Confederation, was the promise contained in that clause of the Terms of Union quoted at the opening of this memorial, and they naturaly expected that a union with the Dominion would bring them uninterrupted communication at all seasons of the year with the rest of Canada and of the world. They believed that they would thereafter enjoy equal facilities for intercourse with the other Provinces as those Provinces enjoyed between themselves, and that thenceforth they would participate in many benefits and advantages accruing from the Intercolonial Railway and other public works upon the Mainland, from which they had previously been debarred for a great portion of the year. Cut off, as they had always been for nearly five months of the twelve, from all communication with the Mainland, except by a most uncertain and dangerous route, the promise of continuous communication with the Intercolonial Railway and the railway system of the Dominion was, indeed, a strong incentive to them to surrender their self-government and unite with Canada.

9. The inconvenience and loss which they have suffered in consequence of the failure of the Dominion Government to provide them with the efficient communication promised, are incalculable, while the disappointment to their reasonable expectations has not tended to enhance in their estimation, the value of a connection with the Dominion, but on the contrary, has awakened a feeling of discontent which, though a matter of regret, is not unnatural under the circumstances. Were it only the transport of frieght and merchandise that was stopped during the winter, they would have good reason to complain of being precluded from the benefits of the Intercolonial and other railways which their more fortunate neighbors on the Mainland enjoy; but their chief grievances is that, in direct violation of the solemn compact upon which they entered Confederation, and to which Your Majesty was graciously pleased to be a party, the Dominion Government have not provided that efficient or continuous means whereby mails and passengers can be transported to and from the Mainland.

10. The peoble of this Province, we submit, have just ground of complaint at the inaction of the Dominion Government, and at the extraordinary apathy which has been shown in regard to the interest of this Island, in the matter of communication with the Mainland. Nine winters have passed since the *Northern Light* was first placed on the route, and, notwithstanding the fact that her inefficiency for the service was apparent from the outset, no other steps have been taken to fulfil the Terms of Union, From the time the *Northern Light* ceases running until she again resumes her trips, a period averaging as already mentioned, sixty-four days each year, the Post Office department transmits the mails by the route between Capes Traverse and Tormentine, and during this period in each year, the Dominion Government have, at no time since Confederation, made any provision whatever, for the transport of passengers, who are forced to make such arrangements as best they can for crossing to and from the Mainland. This unaccountable neglect on the part of the Government of Canada is the most direct violation of the Terms of Union which we are called upon to repre-

sent to Your Majesty. Moreover the Dominion Government have established no communication between the Intercolonial Railay and Cape Tormentine, so that travellers are compelled in passing between these points, to drive in open sleighs a distance of forty miles, in the coldest and most stormy portion of the year. Between Cape Traverse and the line of the Prince Edward Island Railway, a distance of about twelve miles, railway connection has been opened, and that but partially only this winter, although provided for by Parliament three years ago.

11. The derangement of business consequent upon the irregularity of the mail service, when for many days at times no communication is had with the rest of Canada, exercises a most prejudicial effect upon the interests of the Island. The hardships of travelling, which only the strong and robust are able to endure, and the dangers attendant upon the present mode which have been most painfully exemplified this winter, are other disadvantages from which the people of this Province suffer most acutely.

12. The feeling that they are being unjustly treated is not without strong foundation. In order to fulfil the Terms of Union with British Columbia, a province of less than 15,000 of a population, exclusive of Indians and Chinese, Canada has contracted for the construction of nearly three thousand miles of railway at a cost of more than eighty millions of dollars. This gigantic undertaking is being pushed forward at a rate unparalleled in the world's history, and a vast expenditure is being made, and still more is contemplated, in acquiring and subsidizing other railroads and in forging the links to bind the scattered Provinces from the Atlantic to the Pacific; yet the fulfilment of the Terms of Union with this Island, by providing the means of communication over a Strait, only nine miles wide, is postponed from year to year, without any thought, it would seem, that thereby a sacred obligation is being violated, and an immense injury being done to a large body of people.

13. This grievance of which we here complain has been repeatedly brought to the notice of the General Government, while, session after session, the representatives of the Island in the Dominion Parliament have called attention to the non-fulfilment by Canada of her pledged faith with this Island. In 1881 we addressed the Governor General in Council upon the subject, and prayed for the adoption of measures to remedy the state of affairs complained of as well as compensation for the loss sustained on account of the non-fulfilment of the Terms of Union. This address was duly acknowledged, but no practical results followed, and upon the notice of the Dominion Government being again directed thereto, assurances were returned in both of the years 1882 and 1883, that the question was under their consideration. Again last year we addressed His Excellency in Council with a like petition, and claiming five millions of dollars for the loss sustained to that time on account of the non-fulfilment of the said Terms, and we also informed the Dominion Government that we then approached

them for the last time, and that unless a favorable answer was accorded without delay, Your Majesty's interference would be invoked. Beyond a simple acknowledgment of this Address no attention has been paid to it. Again on the 20th February last, the Executive Council of this Island called the attention of the Dominion Government to the various steps which had been taken by the Island to obtain a settlement of the question, and reminded them of the decision at which we had arrived last year to appeal to Your Majesty, and that no alternative was left except to carry that determination into effect. To this Minute the same unsatisfactory answer was received, which has been invariably given. Copies of the correspondence referred to will be transmitted to Your Majesty herewith.

14. In this the twelfth year of their connection with the Dominion, instead of enjoying that efficient and continuous steam communication with the Mainland which was guaranteed them, the people of Prince Edward are, for a very considerable portion of the year, dependent upon the mode which their fathers initiated upwards of sixty years ago, before steam power was ever applied for purposes of locomotion. During these twelve years, they have patiently awaited the fulfilment by the General Government of the Terms of Union in this particular, until we are reluctantly constrained to say that the Dominion Government have evinced a marked indifference not only for the welfare of this Island, but for the sanctity of their own obligation as well.

15. Satisfied that this state of things cannot longer continue without a breach of that harmony which is so indispensable between the Provinces of the Confederation, and feeling that the Island is being treated unjustly, and its prosperity seriously retarded, we appeal to Your Majesty and humbly pray, that You will take the premises into Your most gracious consideration, and require that justice be done by the Government of Canada to Your Majesty's loyal subjects of this Province, by the immediate establishment and maintenance of efficient steam service for the conveyance of mails and passengers between this Island and the Mainland of the Dominion, both winter and summer, so as to place the Island in continuous communication with the Intercolonial Railway and the railway system of the Dominion; and further, that Your Majesty will be pleased to require that the Government of Canada compensate this Island for the loss which has resulted to its inhabitants, by reason of the non-fulfilment of the Terms of Confederation, in the particular complained of herein.

Certified,

JOHN BALL, C. L. C.
FREDERICK W. HUGHES, A. C. H. A.

MESSAGE.

A. A. MACDONALD, Lieutenant Governor.

The Lieutenant Governor transmits to the House of Assembly the accompanying Copies of Despatches and other Documents relating to the Joint Address of the Legislative Council and House of Assembly to Her Majesty the Queen, on the subject of the Terms upon which this Island entered the Confederation.

Government House, April, 28th, 1886.

Extract from Minutes of Executive Council of Prince Edward Island.

COUNCIL CHAMBER,

August 4th, 1885.

The Executive Council in Committee have had under consideration the separate Addresses of the Legislative Council and House of Assembly of this Province to His Honor the Lieutenant Governor, passed during their last Session, requesting that, owing to their unwillingness to embarrass the Government of Canada during the existence of the insurrection in the Northwest Territories, their Joint Memorial to Her Majesty the Queen, praying Her Majesty's most gracious intervention, in order to obtain from the Government of Canada a fulfilment of the Terms upon which this Island entered the Confederation in respect to communication with the Mainland, and also the payment of compensation to this Province for the loss sustained by its people in consequence of the failure of the Dominion Government to carry out the aforesaid Terms, should not be forwarded until such time during the then approaching recess, as in the opinion of His Honor's advisers should be deemed opportune.

The Council in Committee advise that, as the insurrection has been effectually suppressed and order restored in the Northwest Territories, the said Joint Address to Her Majesty the Queen, together with the enclosures therein referred to, the said separate Addresses to His Honor and a copy of this Minute be immediately forwarded to His Excellency the Governor General for transmission to Her Majesty the Queen.

Approved by His Honor the Lieutenant Governor.

Certified, a true Extract,

R. F. DE BLOIS,

Clerk Executive Council.

[COPY.]

GOVERNMENT HOUSE,
Charlottetown, Prince Edward Island,
August 4th, 1885.

SIR:—

I have the honor to forward herewith to His Excellency the Governor General of Canada, for transmission to Her Majesty the Queen, a Joint Address from the Legislative Council and House of Assembly of this Province, praying Her Majesty's most gracious intervention, in order to obtain from the Government of Canada a fulfilment of the Terms upon which this Island entered the Confederation in respect to Communication with the Mainland, and also of compensation to this Province for the loss sustained by its people in consequence of the failure of the Dominion Government to carry out the aforesaid terms. I also enclose copies of the following papers relating to this subject to be forwarded with the said Address:—

Despatch No. 18, of 7th April, 1881, from Lieutenant Governor of Prince Edward Island, to Secretary of State, Ottawa, transmitting Joint Address of both branches of this Legislature to His Excellency the Governor General, praying that immediate measures may be adopted by the Dominion Government to fulfil the Terms of Confederation with this Province. Also a copy of that Address and the acknowledgment of its receipt by the Secretary of State at Ottawa, bearing date 16th April, 1881.

Despatch No. 9, of 28th February, 1882, from the Lieutenant Governor to the Secretary of State, Ottawa, informing him that no reply had been received to the above address, and that this Government is anxious to have the reply with as little delay as possible, also the acknowledgment of the receipt of this despatch by the Secretary of State, dated 8th March, 1882.

Extract from Minutes of the Executive Council of this Island, dated 31st January, 1883, to His Honor the Lieutenant Governor, forwarded by him to the Secretary of State, Ottawa, again bringing the subject to the notice of His Excellency in Council, and requesting a reply to the former address of the Council and Assemby therein referred to.

Telegram dated Charlottetown, 27th March, 1883, from the Lieutenant Governor to the Secretary of State, Ottawa, requesting reply to be laid before the Legislature, then in session, with acknowledgment from the Secretary of State, informing the Lieutenant Governor that the subject was under consideration.

Despatch No. 8, of 18th April, 1884, from the Lieutenant Governor, transmitting a Joint Address of the Legislative Council and House of Assembly of the Province, to His Excellency the Governor General, again representing the failure of the Dominion

Government to carry out part of the Terms of Confederation, and praying that His Excellency the Governor General in Council will take such action as shall cause this grievance to be remedied, and also that compensation be paid to this Island for non-fulfilment of said terms, with the Joint Address referred to, and the Despatch No. 1770, of 24th April, 1884, from the Under Secretary of State, Ottawa, acknowledging receipt thereof, and stating that the matter will receive due consideration.

Despatch No. 27, of 28th February, 1885, from the Lieutenant Governor to the Secretary of State, Ottawa, transmitting for the consideration of His Excellency the Governor General in Council an approved Minute of Council on the non-fulfilment of the Terms of Confederation, with Minute therein mentioned, and Despatch No. 1788, dated Ottawa 6th March, 1885, acknowledging receipt of the above.

Address from the Legislative Council, and another from the House of Assembly of this Province at the last Session to the Lieutenant Governor with respect to the transmission of the Joint Address, then passed by both branches of the Legislature to Her Majesty the Queen.

Extract from the Minutes of the Executive Council of this Island, dated the 4th August, 1885, advising for the reason therein stated, that the Joint Address of both branches of the Legislature to Her Majesty the Queen, together with the enclosures therein referred to, and the separate Addresses to the Lieutenant Governor from the Provincial Legislative Council and House of Assembly, and the Minute of Council in connection therewith, be immediately forwarded to His Excellency the Governor General for transmission to Her Majesty the Queen.

I have the honor to be,

Sir,

Your obedient Servant,

(Signed), A. A. MACDONALD,

Lieutenant Governor.

The Honorable

The Secretary of State, Ottawa.

3028
on
3993

OTTAWA, August 10th, 1885.

SIR:—

I have the honor to acknowledge the receipt of your despatch of the 4th instant, transmitting a Joint Address to Her Majesty the Queen from the Legislative Council and House of Assembly of Prince Edward Island on the subject of Communication with the Mainland, together with other documents relative thereto, and specified in your despatch.

I have the honor to be,

Sir,

Your obedient servant,

(Signed) G. POWELL,
Under Secretary of State.

His Honor
The Lieutenant Governor of
Prince Edward Island, Charlottetown.

Extract from Minutes of Executive Council of Prince Edward Island.

COUNCIL CHAMBER,

January 14th, 1886.

The Executive Council in Committee have had under consideration the Memorial to Her Most Gracious Majesty the Queen, unanimously adopted by the Legislative Council and House of Assembly, in the Session of 1885, representing the great loss which has accrued to the people of this Province in consequence of the failure of the Dominion Government to fulfil that portion of the Terms of Confederation which guaranteed the "establishment and maintenance of efficient Steam Service for the conveyance of Mails and Passengers between this Island and the Mainland of the Dominion, both winter and summer, so as to place the Island in continuous communication with the Intercolonial Railway and the Railway systems of the Dominion;" as also the Minute of the Executive Council of the 4th of August, 1885, upon the same subject.

Whereupon the Executive Council in Committee recommended that a Delegation be appointed to proceed immediately to the Colonial Office in London for the purpose of supporting the prayer of the said Memorial.

They further recommended that the Honorable William W. Sullivan, Premier and Attorney General, and the Honorable Donald Ferguson, Provincial Secretary, do compose the said Delegation, and the Committee request that Your Honor will be pleased to inform His Excellency the Governor General of such appointment, in order that the Delegates may be provided with an introduction to Her Majesty's Principal Secretary of State for the Colonies, and that Your Honor will also be pleased to ask

His Excellency the Governor General to inform the Right Honorable the Secretary of State for the Colonies of the appointment of such Delegation.

Approved by His Honor the Lieutenant Governor.

Certified, a true Extract,

R. F. DEBLOIS,

Clerk Executive Council.

Extract from Minutes of the Executive Council of Prince Edward Island.

COUNCIL CHAMBER,

January 14th, 1886.

At a meeting of the Executive Council in Committee.

Referring to the Report of the Committee of the Executive Council of this date, approved by His Honor the Lieutenant Governor, appointing the Honorable William W. Sullivan, Premier and Attorney General, and the Honorable Donald Ferguson, Provincial Secretary, a Delegation to proceed to London to support the prayer of the Memorial to Her Majesty the Queen, adopted by the Legislative Council and House of Assembly, in the Session of 1885, relative to the non-fulfilment, by the Dominion Government, of the Terms of Confederation, in respect to Steam Communication between this Island and the Mainland of the Dominion, the Executive Council in Committee recommend that Your Honor do communicate by telegraph to the Right Honorable the Secretary of State for the Colonies, a notification of the appointment of the said Delegation, at the same time soliciting that Her Majesty's decision may be deferred until the Delegates shall have had an opportunity of being heard in support of the prayer of the Memorial; and also that Your Honor inform His Excellency the Governor General of the transmission of such Despatch, and request that His Excellency will likewise be pleased to telegraph to the Right Honorable the Secretary of State for the Colonies asking that Her Majesty's decision may be so deferred.

Approved by His Honor the Lieutenant Governor.

Certified, a true Extract,

R. F. DE BLOIS,

Clerk Executive Council.

[Copy.]

[TELEGRAMS.]

CHARLOTTETOWN, 16th January, 1886.

To Colonial Secretary, London:

Government desire to notify you that Delegates proceed immediately to London to support prayer of Memorial of Legislature respecting non-fulfilment of Terms of Confederation by Canadian Government, and request that the decision be deferred to afford opportunity of their being heard.

(Signed) A. A. MACDONALD,
Lieutenant Governor
Prince Edward Island

LONDON, January 26th, 1886.

To Lieutenant Governor, Prince Edward Island:

Yours Sixteenth; do not perceive Queen can be advised that she has any power to give decision, or direct or enforce action in this case.

(Signed) STANLEY.

[COPY.]

GOVERNMENT HOUSE,
Charlottetown, P. E. Island,
January 18th, 1886.

SIR:—

I have the honor to transmit herewith an approved Minute of my Council, bearing date the 14th January, instant, upon the question of communication between this Island and the Mainland, stipulated for in the Terms of Confederation, and recommending that a Delegation composed of the Honorable W. W. Sullivan, Premier and Attorney General, and the Honorable Donald Ferguson, Provincial Secretary, be appointed to proceed immediately to the Colonial Office in London for the purpose of supporting the prayer of the Memorial on that subject to Her Most Gracious Majesty the Queen, adopted by the Legislative Council and House of Assembly of this Island, in the Session of 1885, and also requesting me to inform His Excellency the Governor General of such appointment, in order that the Delegates may be provided with an introduction to Her Majesty's Principal Secretary of State for the Colonies, and that he may be informed of the appointment of such Delegation.

I have also enclosed herewith, a further approved Minute of my Council bearing the same date, referring to the appointment of such Delegation, and recommending me to communicate by telegraph to the Right Honorable the Secretary of State for the Colonies, a notification of the appointment of such Delegation, and at the same time soliciting that Her Majesty's decision may be deferred until the Delegates shall have had an opportunity of being heard in support of the prayer of the Memorial, which despatch has been forwarded, and recommending me to inform His Excellency the Governor General of the transmission of such despatch, and to request that His

Excellency will likewise be pleased to telegraph the Right Honorable the Secretary of State for the Colonies, asking that Her Majesty's decision may be deferred.

I have the honor to be,

Sir,

Your obedient servant,

(Signed) A. A. MACDONALD,

Lieutenant Governor.

The Honorable

The Secretary of State, Ottawa.

542
on
2014.

[COPY.]

SIR:— OTTAWA, January 23rd, 1886.

I have the honor to acknowledge the receipt of your despatch of the 18th inst., transmitting an approved Minute of your Executive Council, bearing date the 14th January, inst., upon the subject of Communication between Prince Edward Island and the Mainland, stipulated for in the terms of Confederation, and recommending the appointment of a delegation to proceed to England in support of the prayer of the Memorial, together with a further approved Minute of your Council, bearing the same date, referring to the appointment of such delegation, &c., and to state that the matter will receive consideration.

I have the honor to be,

Sir,

Your obedient servant,

(Signed) G. POWELL,

Under Secretary of State.

His Honor

The Lieutenant Governor of

Prince Edward Island, Charlottetown.

724
on
2014

[COPY.]

SIR:— OTTAWA, 28th January, 1886.

With reference to previous correspondence upon the subject of the appointment of a delegation composed of the Honorable W. W. Sullivan, Premier and Attorney General, and the Honorable Donald Ferguson, Provincial Secretary of Prince Edward

Island, to proceed immediately to the Colonial Office in London, for the purpose of supporting the prayer of the Memorial to Her Most Gracious Majesty the Queen, adopted by the Legislative Council and the House of Assembly of the Island, at the session of 1885, with respect to the question of Communication between Prince Edward Island and the Mainland, I have the honor to acquaint you for the information of your Government, that His Excellency the Governor General in Council, has been advised to transmit your despatch of the 18th ultimo, and its enclosures, to the Right Honorable the Secretary of State for the Colonies, and to furnish the delegates with the required letter of introduction to Colonel Stanley.

I have the honor to be,

Sir,

Your obedient servant,

(Signed) J. A. CHAPLEAU,

Secretary of State.

His Honor

The Lieutenant Governor of

Prince Edward Island, Charlottetown.

619
on
2014

[Copy.]

Department of the Secretary of State, Canada,

Ottawa, January 28th, 1886.

Sir:—

I have the honor to acquaint you that His Excellency the Governor General has had under his consideration in Council, a Despatch from His Honor the Lieutenant Governor of Prince Edward Island, dated the 18th January last, transmitting a copy of an improved Minute of his Executive Council, in which it is set forth that a delegation composed of yourself and the Honorable Donald Ferguson, Provincial Secretary, had been appointed to proceed immediately to the Colonial Office in London, for the purpose of supporting the prayer of the Memorial to Her Majesty the Queen, adopted by the Legislative Council and House of Assembly of the Island during the Session of 1885, with respect to the question of communication between Prince Edward Island and the Mainland.

I have now to inform you that His Excellency has been advised to carry into effect the several requests contained in the Despatch and enclosure referred to.

In compliance with His Honor's request I now enclose a letter from His

Excellency to Her Majesty's Principal Secretary of State for the Colonies, introducing the delegation to that Minister.

I have the honor to be,
Sir,
Your obedient servant,

(Signed) J. A. CHAPLEAU,
Secretary of State.

Hon. W. W. Sullivan,
Attorney General of Prince Edward Island,
London, England.

[COPY.]

GOVERNMENT HOUSE,
Ottawa, 27th January, 18[illegible].

SIR:—

I have the honor of introducing to you the Honorable William W. Sullivan, Premier and Attorney General, and the Honorable Donald Ferguson, Provincial Secretary of the Province of Prince Edward Island, who have been appointed a delegation on behalf of the Government of that Province to proceed to London for the purpose of supporting the case of Prince Edward Island against the Dominion in the matter of Steam Communication between the Island and the Mainland.

I have the honor to be,
Sir,
Your most obedient humble servant,

(Signed) LANDSDOWNE.

Colonel,
The Right Honorable
Frederick A. Stanley, &c., &c.

[COPY.]

COLONIAL OFFICE,
February 23rd, 1886.

MY DEAR SIR:—

Lord Granville will be happy to see you and Mr. Ferguson here at 4 p. m., to-morrow, Wednesday, on the subject of the Address from Prince Edward Island to the Queen.

Yours sincerely,

(Signed) ROBERT G. W. HERBERT.

The Honorable,
W. W. Sullivan, &c., &c., &c.

Certified Copy of a Report of a Committee of the Honorable the Privy Council for Canada, approved by His Excellency the Governor General in Council, on the 7th Day of November, 1885.

The Committee of the Privy Council have had under consideration a Despatch, dated 4th August, 1885, from the Lieutenant Governor of Prince Edward Island, transmitting Joint Addresses of the Legislative Council and House of Assembly of that Province to Her Majesty the Queen, praying Her intervention on behalf of Prince Edward Island to obtain from the Dominion Government a fulfilment of its engagement "to maintain efficient steam service for the conveyance of mails and passengers between the Island and the Mainlanland, summer and winter."

The Committee advise that Your Excellency be moved to forward the aforesaid Joint Addresses of the Legislative Council and Assembly of Prince Edward Island to to Her Majesty the Queen.

The Committee concurring in the report herewith of the sub-Committe of Council to whom the despatch and enclosures were referred, further advise that a copy of this Minute and of the annexed report, if approved, be forwarded, together with a copy of the said Joint Addresses to the Right Honorable the Secretary of State for the Colonies.

All which is respectfully submitted for Your Excellency's approval.

(Signed) JOHN J. McGEE,
Clerk Privy Council, Canada.

(Copy)

Your sub-Committee find that the Government of Prince Edward Island previous to Confederation subsidized two steamers for the conveyance of mails and passengers to and from the Mainland during the summer season, and that for a period of five months or more mails were carried by ice-boats from Cape Traverse to Cape Tormentine, and thence by sleigh to Amherst, the land carriage being fifty-two miles, and from Cape to Cape over ice and water, nine miles.

Since the Union a subsidy of ten thousand dollars a year has been paid by the Dominion Government to the Prince Edward Island Steam Navigation Company to run steamers daily during the season of open navigation from Shediac in New Brunswick, to Summerside in the Island, and from Pictou in Nova Scotia, to Charlottetown and Georgetown. This service has been regularly and satisfactorily maintained by that Company, but as their steamers have to lay up early in the fall, the Dominion Government steamer *Northern Light* then takes up the service and continues it as long as the ice permits.

Previous to the Union paddle-wheel steamers only were employed, and it was very generally believed, and for good reasons, that a screw steamer would maintain steam communication to a much later period, but it is altogether improbable that any man who had seen the Straits of Northumberland, or had any knowledge of the ice obstruction in mid-winter, could have supposed it possible to construct a steamer capable of crossing when the ice is at its heaviest in that season, and it is proper to assume that both contracting parties to the Union having such knowledge, understood that the Dominion Government would provide and maintain the means which science and experience might determine as the best and most efficient for the end in view, within the range of possibility.

The Dominion Government, willing and most anxious to do all it was possible in the interests of Prince Edward Island, in the season next following the Union sought by public advertisements for persons to undertake the service, and eventually secured a contract for ten years with a Mr. King who claimed to have a steamer specially fitted for ice work. She proved, however, unable to run longer than until the fourth of January On the part of Mr. King it was claimed that the season was of unusual severity, and by the inhabitants of Prince Edward Island it was alleged that the steamer was wanting in power and of a model unsuited to the service.

The contract after this trial was cancelled, and the Dominion Government after the most careful and anxious enquiry, contracted with a Mr. Sewell, of Quebec, to complete a powerful steamer on a model specially designed for ice service.

In December, 1876, this steamer named the *Northern Light* was completed and placed upon the route between Pictou and Charlottetown, and has been maintained each winter to date at an aggregate cost including construction of $249,956.57.

As was feared, the *Northern Light* has been, during the severest part of the winters, unable to force a way through the enormous fields of ice which block the Straits at that season, but whilst demonstrating fully the impossibility of continuous steam communication in mid-winter has reduced the period of interruption to an average of one-third of that previous to the Union.

In the Session of the Dominion Parliament of 1883, a Committe of the House of Commons composed of three representatives from Prince Edward Island, and two fom the Mainland, was appointed on the 23rd February to investigate the question of steam communication with the Island. All the members of the Committee had personal knowledge of the obstruction to navigation in the Straits by ice in winter, and were well qualified for the duty assigned to them.

After long and careful consideration of the subject and examination "of persons, papers and records," the Committee reported on 18th April, 1883, in the following words: "It is the unanimous opinion of the members of Committee, confirmed by the testimony of witnesses of large practical experience, that no steamships can be built capable of keeping up continuous communication in mid-winter." The following extract from their Report set this forth more at large:—

"House of Commons Committee Room,

"18th April, 1883.

"Your Committee beg leave to report as follows:—

"When Prince Edward Island was admitted into the Union, the following was one of the stipulations on the part of the Dominion Government contained in the Terms of Union.

"Efficient Steam Service for the conveyance of Mails and Passengers, to be established and maintained between the Island and the Dominion, winter and summer, thus placing the Island in continuous communication with the Intercolonial Railway and the Railway system of the Dominion.

"This communication has been maintained in the summer season by the Prince Edward Island Steam Navigation Company between Summerside and Shediac, and between Charlottetown and Pictou, calling at Georgetown; and in the winter season by the *Northern Light* between Georgetown and Pictou, and by ice boats between Capes Traverse and Tormentine.

"To determine the efficiency of this service in the past, and how communication may be most regularly and efficiently maintained in the future, the Committee carefully examined the records of the trips made by the *Northern Light* during the seasons she has been on the route; also summoned and examined some of the officers in charge, and find that she performed the following number of trips, and failed the number of days marked opposite each season.

* * * * * * * * *

"That on an average there were forty-eight days in midwinter she was unable to effect the crossing.

"The daily records kept by the Captain of the *Northern Light*, and the testimony given by the officers, show that the heavy ice encountered was the cause which compelled him to discontinue crossing in mid-winter.

"The evidence of the officers examined is also to the effect that the steamer is not sufficient to overcome the difficulties of the winter navigation, and although they suggest slight improvements on her model, which would better fit her for the purposes for which she was intended, still are unanimously of opinion that no steamship can be built capable of keeping up continuous communication in mid-winter between the Island the Mainland.

"We examined personally several gentlemen of large practical experience in crossing from the Island in the winter season, all of whom confirm the above, and whose evidence is hereto appended."

The Committee having reached this conclusion made certain suggestions for the improvements of the route by the Capes, the most important of which, viz.: the construction of lines of railway to the Capes, and suitable shipping piers had been previously decided upon by th Dominion Government.

The Address points out that the distance from the Intercolonial Railway to Cape Tormentine is forty miles, and from the Island Railway to Cape Traverse, twelve miles, which it is stated had to be travelled "in open sleighs in the coldest and most stormy portion of the year, "but omits to state that a Railway to Cape Tormentine was under construction, and a large sum provided for the erection of a shipping pier, whilst to Cape Traverse, on the Island side, the railway had been completed, and as suggested by the Committee of Parliament, houses of shelter for passengers, boatmen and boats, had been erected.

The language of the Address in alleging that the Dominion Government has "shown no sufficient disposition to fulfil its obligations towards the Island," and with having "unaccountably neglected and treated with apathy and indifference" the interests of the Island, seems to the undersigned in view of all the circumstances unwarranted.

For half a century the Government of Prince Edward Island forwarded mails and passengers by ice-boats across the Straits and by open sleighs overland for five months in each year, and more recently by subsidized steamers in summer, instead of sailing packets.

This change from sailing vessels to steamers for summer appears to have been the only change or improvement made by the Island Government in fifty-years although having control of a larger sum in revenue than the Island now pays into the Dominion Treasury.

The efforts of the Dominion Government, as marked by expenditure to meet the wishes of the people of Prince Edward Island and to give them improved means of communication with the Mainland, are of course known to the Legislative Council and House of Assembly, although they have been overlooked by them when preparing the Address. That expenditure may be summarily stated as follows:—

Cost and Maintenance of *Northern Light*	$249,956.57
Subsidies for Summer Service and for ice-boats at Capes	196,073.75
Construction of Cape Traverse Branch Railway and enlargement of Pier	199,190.03
Expended by Public Works Department in connection with Piers, Boat-houses and Cable Service	25,678.53
To pay Island Government for Pier required in Cape Service	12,400.00
Subsidy for construction of Railway to Cape Tormentine	118,400.00

Appropriation for Pier at Cape Tormentine.. 150,000.00

Total........................ ....$951,698.00

This large expenditure for the transmission, in comfort of passengers to and from the Capes, is worthy of more consideration in view of the fact that in the last two seasons the average number of passengers in each crossing of the *Northern Light* was only a fraction over nine, and of the further fact that the Dominion Government has maintained the Island Railway at a cost since its opening to 30th June, 1884, of $843,911 in excess of all its receipts, besides an expenditure thereon on capital account of about half a million of dollars.

The passenger list of the *Northern Light* for the winters 1884 5 averaging only nine per trip, and the large annual deficit in working the Island Railway, are the best evidence of the limited travel to be provided for, and although it may be some inconvenience to have steam communication suspended for a period of 48 days, yet it does not warrant the language of the Address that "an incalculable loss has been suffered by the people of Prince Edward Island by the failure of the Dominion Government" to do what a Committee of Parliament says is impossible.

In the accompanying Address passed by the Legislature in 1884, it is claimed that the loss is great because the chief pursuit of the Island people is agriculture, and the compensation for damages is placed at five million dollars as due to the date of the Address.

In considering this assertion it must be borne in mind that the Dominion Government did not undertake the carrying of agricultural produce nor freight of any kind, although it has at all times afforded facilities for the transport of any freight offering.

It is further stated in the Address that Prince Edward Island has been unjustly and invidiously treated, in as much as the Dominion Government has contracted at a cost of many millions of dollars "for 3,000 miles of a railway to British Columbia, a Province with 10,000 of a population, exclusive of Indians and Chinese, whilst in the case of Prince Edward Island, a sacred obligation is being violated and an immense injury done to a large body of people."

The undersigned cannot refrain from submitting that a discussion of the relative importance of the several Provinces, and of the comparative expenditure therein of the Federal moneys, is not the means best adapted to promote that harmony which the Address of 1884 says is so "indispensible between the Provinces of the Confederation."

In the distribution of public moneys Prince Edward Island has no cause of complaint. It is true that large expenditures have been made for Railways and Canals in the general interest, but the local wants of the Provinces have not been overlooked, and Prince Edward Island has been dealt with in a most liberal manner and apparently without regard to her contribution to the revenue.

The Address seeks in its reference to the construction of the Canadian Pacific Railway an opportunity to establish and emphasize a wrong to Prince Edward Island. Doubtless the maintenance of continuous steam communication between the Island and the Mainland in mid-winter, is of as much interest to the people of that Province as is the construction of the Canadian Pacific Railway, although in the one case it means the transport of nine passengers a day for an average period of forty-eight days a year in mid-winter, whilst in the other it is a great national work, providing a highway in common for the Eastern and Western Provinces, and the opening up of vast areas of the richest soil upon which many settlers from the older Provinces, including Prince Edward Island, are finding homes, instead of in the United States. To take the view indicated by the Address, that the construction of the Canadian Pacific Railway is merely a local work, the comparison then suggested with Prince Edward Island should not be confined to British Columbia, as Ontario, Manitoba and the North-West Territories receive as much local benefit therefrom as does British Columbia.

In a strictly local view it is not unjust to say that expenditure shall, in some measure, be governed by receipts, present or prospective, and the tone of the Legislature of Prince Eward Island in speaking, in 1884, of "British Columbia" as a "Province of 10,000 people, exclusive of Indians and Chinese," and in 1885 "of 15,000," demands a comparison of revenue returns from the two provinces.

"In the returns last published, 30th June, 1884, Prince Edward Island is credited with—

From Customs	$170,863.40
" Excise	22,615.26
Total contribution to revenue	$193,478.66

In the same year British Columbia is credited with—

From Customs	$884,076.21
" Excise	58,018.89
Total contribution to revenue	$942,095.10

Nearly five times as much as Prince Edward Island in the comparison which is called for by the reference to the Canadian Pacific Railway. In the Address Manitoba and the North-West Territories should be included as follows:

From Customs	$734,185.77
" Excise	157,417.99
	$891,683.76
Total revenue contributed by British Columbia, Manitoba and the North-West Territories	$1,833,698.86
As against Prince Edward Island	193,478.66

If evidence were wanting of the anxious desire of the Dominion Government to promote the interests of Prince Edward Island in every possible way, it may be found in the same public returns of the expenditure in and for the Island in 1884, which is by no means exceptional, viz:

Payment of interest on her public debt		$195,407.55
Subsidy to Local Government for local purposes		164,510.00
Postal expenses	$46,465.21	
Less Postal Revenue	29,154.80	
		17,310.41
Expenses of operating Railway in excess of revenue receipts		91,924.01
Militia and Defence		12,141.00
Collection of Customs		20,856.21
Collection of Excise		2,506.89
Administration of Justice		18,800.00
Maintenance of Lights and Buoys		19,059.62
Protection of Fisheries and Fish Breeding, exclusive of bounty payments		3,539.38
Superannuation		2,156.00
Lieutenant Governor's Salary		7,000.00
Subsidies to Steamers and Winter Service		32,876.00
Subsidy to Fishwick's Steamboat		3,000.00
Outside Expenses—Lights		3,000.00
Indians		1,993.87
Public Health		885.40
Audit and Assistant Receiver General's Offices		4,845.92
Subsidy to Telegraph Connection		1,946.66
Expenditure on Harbors and Rivers		28,581.88
Public Buildings		7,861.89
Construction of Lights		2,158.60
Interest upon a capital expenditure on Island Railway of $578,920		28,946.00
Relief of Sick Seamen	$1,226.31	
Less Dues	684.46	
		541.85
Expenditure by Department of Agriculture		1,389.88
Representation, say		15,000.00
Repairs of Dredges		1,714.99
Total		$689,954.91

It will thus be observed that while the expenditure for the fiscal year ended, 30th June, 1884, is $689,954.91, the total revenue derived from all sources is but $193,478.66, making an expenditure of over $6 per head of the population (112,000), of the Island, whilst the total receipts are only $1.72 per head. It will be claimed, on behalf of the Island, that the population consumes goods the produce of the Mainland. No doubt this is true, but the same occurred previous to the Confederation.

In 1872 the imports of the Colony of Prince Edward Island from the Dominion were:

From Old Canada...$381,179.00

From Nova Scotia	358,961.00
" New Brunswick	327,340.00
Total	$1,067,480.00

Upon which duties were collected.

The total entered for consumption from all countries was	$1,605,241.00
And the total revenue	302,757.00

The total exports of the Colony were	$1,497,058.00
Of which Nova Scotia and New Brunswick took	$749,129.00

Or say one-half.

No doubt the same Inter-Provincial trade continues, with this change in favor of Prince Edward Island, that the goods from the other Provinces are now free of duty, whilst previous to the Union they paid duties the same as on importations from other countries. That Prince Edward Island may have felt inconvenience from the interruption in the trips of the *Northern Light*, may be admitted; but that her material interests have suffered greatly is disproved by the fact that her exports to foreign countries have nearly doubled from 1872 to 1884, whilst the increase of the whole Dominion for the same period has been only ten and a half per cent.

In making this comparison of the payments to the general revenues by Prince Edward Island and British Columbia, and the North-West Territories, and in stating the annual expenditure for the Island, the undersigned are moved thereto only by the implied charge on the Address, that the Western Provinces are being treated by the Dominion Government more generously than the Island, and it is not intended that the liberal manner in which all the public services of the Island have been dealt with, regardless of the revenue receipts, shall be taken as a consideration or recompense for the alleged failure to carry out the Terms of Union.

The liberal treatment of Prince Edward Island results from the policy and practice of the Dominion Government to watch over the interests of the smaller Provinces, and Prince Edward Island, from her isolated position, and with a population less than some cities on the Mainland, has received especial consideration.

If continuous Steam Communication has not been maintained, it is certainly not because the Dominion Government sought to avoid expense. The *Northern Light* is as large and powerful a steamer as experience in Arctic exploration has proved advisable, and she is kept on full expense, equipped and ready to run at all times during the entire winter, and were it possible to do so, no additional expense would be incurred except for fuel, whilst the cost of the Iceboat service would be saved, and the construction of Railways, Piers and Boat-houses to and at the Capes, Traverse and Tormentine, rendered unnecessary.

It is stated in the Addresses that "beyond the formal acknowledgments of memorials from the Island Government, no other answers were given;" but the action taken by the Dominion Government was a better answer than any paper declaration.

The *Northern Light* was constructed and placed at Charlottetown as head quarters. Her officers and crew are inhabitants of the Island, and her unceasing and hazardous efforts to make communication in the severest weather cannot be unknown to the Island Government. The representatives of the Island were in Parliament when appropriations were made for the construction of the Railway to Cape Traverse, and for the erection of piers.

It was publicly known that a Railway was under construction to Cape Tormentine, where the Dominion Government had appropriated $150,000 to erect a suitable shipping pier in connection with the road (to hasten the completion of which a subsidy of $118,400 has now been granted), and that Boat-houses had been erected at the Capes, as recommended by the Committee of Parliament hereinbefore referred to. That the Island Government was fully conversant with the whole action and plans of the Dominion Government, may be assumed from the fact that it demanded payment of $12,400 for an old public wharf that was utilized in the construction of the pier at Cape Traverse.

In brief, the Island Government knew that every possible effort had been made by the Dominion Government to navigate the Straits from Charlottetown and Georgetown to Pictou, with a failure of an average of forty-eight days; it knew that the Dominion Government, in making great expenditures on railway lines to the Capes, was most anxious to reorganize and improve, if possible, that route, notwithstanding that in the ordinary annual local services of the Island the Dominion Government was returning more than three dollars for every dollar received.

All of which is respectfully submitted.

(Signed) A. W. McLELAN.
(Signed) A. CAMPBELL.

LONDON, March 1st, 1886.

MY LORD:—

The undersigned having, at the interview with which your Lordship honored them on Wednesday last, been favored by your Lordship with a copy of a Report of a Committee of the Honorable the Privy Council of Canada upon the Joint Address of the Legislative Council and House of Assembly of Prince Edward Island to Her Majesty the Queen, on the subject of the non-fulfilment, by the Dominion Government, of the Terms of Union with respect to communication between the Island and the Mainland of Canada, desire to offer the following comments thereon:—

Your Lordship, whose successful administration of Colonial affairs is well remembered in the Dominion, in a despatch to Sir John Young, Governor-General of

Canada, dated 4th September, 1869, when commending the action of the Dominion Government in re-opening negotiations with the Island, with a view to its admission into the Confederation, used the following words:—

"I trust that in settling the Terms proposed as the basis of this arrangement, the Government will deal liberally as well as justly with the Island."

The undersigned deeply regret that it has been found necessary to appeal to Her Majesty to obtain that justice, in the carrying out of the Terms agreed upon, which has hitherto been denied the Island.

The Committee of the Privy Council of Canada give it as their opinion "that it is altogether improbable that any man who had seen the Straits of Northumberland, or had any knowledge of the ice obstruction in mid-winter, could have supposed it possible to construct a steamer capable of crossing when the ice is at its heaviest in that season."

The undersigned submit that the offer of continuous steam communication, summer and winter, was an entirely voluntary act on the part of the Dominion, made in 1869, when Canada endeavored, at the instance of the Imperial Government, to induce Prince Edward Island to enter the Confederation, to which the inhabitants of the Island had previously been strongly opposed. The Terms of Union then proposed were rejected by the Island, but upon a more favorable basis, in other respects, the Union was effected on 1st July, 1873, the conditions containing the same stipulation for continuous communication as were offered in 1869. The undersigned have every reason to believe that the terms were concluded in good faith, and they submit that such terms should be carried out. Ample time has been afforded since the consummation of the Union, to effect this communication, yet the undersigned must repeat the language of the Memorial to Her Majesty, that "no sufficient disposition has been shown by the Dominion Government to fulfil their obligations towards the Island in this matter."

The first steamer which was engaged to attempt the crossing between Georgetown and Pictou was notoriously unfit, as the Committee of Council acknowledge. She possessed no qualification for the service, having been originally employed as a wood-boat, and not having been constructed to receive steam machinery. After remaining on the route for two seasons, the Government were obliged to cancel the contract with her owner. The *Northern Light, which was not designed for the service*, was purchased by the Government in 1876, and placed upon the route; her incapacity for the work was early made manifest, and has been patent to the Government for many years, yet no steps have been taken to substitute a more efficient vessel, or to supplement her with another steamer. Here the undersigned would call attention to a speech in the Senate, in 1884, wherein Sir Alexander Campbell, one of the Sub-Committee, whose names are signed to the report now under review, promised that a second steamer would be placed on the route to assist the *Northern Light*. Sir Alexander made use of the following language:—

"The notice that the honorable gentleman from Charlottetown has given is that he will call the attention of the Government to the expediency of making timely preparation for replacing the steamship *Northern Light* by a new vessel, combining such improvements in design and construction as modern experience dictates. In reply to the inquiry, I may say that the Marine Department has entered into a contract for the building of a wooden screw steamer for light-house service in the Maritime Provinces and it is intended to build this vessel with extra strong timbers, sheath her with green-heart, and plate her bows with steel or iron, so as to fit her for ice navigation, and to assist the *Northern Light* when necessary. She will be ready for service in October next. It is also intended to repair the *Northern Light* thoroughly, next season, replacing all defective timbers and planks, and otherwise strengthening the vessel and fitting her thoroughly for winter navigation. There would then be, therefore, for the service of the Government in or near these Straits, the *Northern Light*, thoroughly restored and strengthened, and this new vessel which is now being constructed, and which is to be finished in October, so that the valuable suggestions of my honorable friend would be acted upon, and there would be another vessel there in the event of an accident happening to one of them."

Strange as it may seem, the new vessel has never been employed to assist the *Northern Light*, although the latter was unavailable for service last winter from the 26th January till the 28th April, a period of ninety-one days.

It is true that a branch railway has been built to Cape Traverse, but it was not completed until January 1885, nearly three years after the appropriation for its construction, and nearly twelve years after the Island entered the Union. A pier has also been constructed at that point, but until some natural obstructions are removed, it is available only for vessels of light draught, and a steamer cannot lie at it. A branch railway is also in course of construction to Cape Tormentine in New Brunswick, but it is, even at this date, only about one half finished, and, being in the hands of a private Company, there is no certainty when it will be completed, notwithstanding that the Dominion Government have voted a subsidy to the undertaking. An appropriation was also made, some years ago, for the construction of a pier at Cape Tormentine, but, up to the present time, so far as is known to the undersigned, the site even has not been finally determined, and no attempt has ever been made to run a steamer, at any season, between Capes Traverse and Tormentine.

The Committee of Council assume that the Island Government were fully conversant with the whole action and plans of the Dominion Government towards improving the winter communication, yet the undersigned have reason to believe that the Dominion Government themselves were not fully advised of what was being done in the matter. Although a Committee of Parliament, in 1883, recommended the erection of boathouses at both Capes, for the accommodation of the men engaged in the service, and for the shelter of the boats, they were not finished until the winter of this year. Sir Alexander Campbell, speaking in the Senate, in 1884, said:—

"I am surprised to hear from my honorable friend opposite that the boathouses have not been built. I called the attention of the Minister of Marine (Mr. McLelan) to the matter last Session, and he told me that the boathouses would be provided. I shall again call his attention to that question, and to the various suggestions that have been made."

Again, in the Parliamentary Session of 1885, Sir Alexander Campbell, speaking on the same subject, said:—

"My honorable friend from Prince Edward Island, who introduced this subject to the notice of the House, has, I think, just ground for complaint—ground for complaint, I am sorry to think, perhaps against myself, although really, as he has almost admitted, I am not responsible for the non-execution of the measures which, from time to time, I have been authorized by the Government to promise in this House. I remember quite distinctly the undertaking which I gave that the boathouses should be constructed, one on each side of the ferry. I made that promise with the authority of the then Minister of Marine and Fisheries, and as is my constant practice, the very day the promise was made, I wrote to the Minister of Marine and Fisheries, that, pursuant to what he had told me, I made the promise, and that I hoped he would keep it in mind. I afterwards called attention to it, and there were reasons which were more or less sound—I can hardly say sound—which made the delay more or less excusable. It was thought for a time that the orders had been given, and that the boathouses were in course of construction."

The Dominion Government have totally neglected, ever since Confederation, to make any provision whatever for the transport of passengers, when compelled to resort to the Capes' route. While the contract with the ice-couriers stipulated for the carriage of mails, no arrangements were made for passengers, who were forced to effect the crossing as best they could, although the Terms of Union require like provision to be made for passengers as for mails. The undersigned would remark that the benefits conferred by the Branch Railway to Cape Traverse are very questionable, when it is understood that, after landing passengers at that point, the Government made no arrangements for carry them across the Straits.

Nearly thirteen years have elapsed since the Island became a member of the Confederation, and all that has been accomplished in the fulfilment of the guarantee to provide continuous communication has been the purchase, for the Georgetown-Pictou route, of a steamer, which, during the last five years, has been laid up an average of *seventy days* each winter, and the completion, on the Capes' route, of a Branch Railroad twelve miles in length, only a small part of the distance intervening between the Island Railway and the Intercolonial Railway. Even the promises made by a Minister of the Crown (Sir Alexander Campbell) have received only tardy fulfilment, and his assurance that a steamer should be employed to assist the *Northern Light* has never been carried out.

Referring to the Report of the Committee of Parliament, in the Session of 1883, to investigate the question of steam communication with the Island, the Committee of Council say that, after long and careful consideration of the subject, and examination of persons, papers, and records, the Parliamentary Committee reported, on the 18th April, 1883, in the following words:—

"It is the unanimous opinion of the Members of Committee, confirmed by the testimony of witnesses of large practical experience, that no steamships can be built capable of keeping up continuous communication in midwinter."

The undersigned have examined the Report of the said Parliamentary Committee, and have failed to discover therein that they came to this conclusion.

The Island Legislature, in their Memorial to Her Majesty, having instanced the anxiety of the Dominion to fulfil its obligations to British Columbia, by the construction, at an enormous cost, of the Canadian Pacific Railway, as contrasted with the apathy and neglect exhibited in carrying out its pledged faith with Prince Edward Island, in the matter of continuous communication, the Committee of Council proceed to institute a comparison between the amounts contributed to the general revenue by British Columbia and Prince Edward Island, stating them at $942,095.10 and $193,478.66 respectively.

Before proceeding to remark upon this point, the undersigned desire to submit that the question of comparative contributions, on either side, is one altogether apart from the issue in this case, which is simply one of performing the term of a most solemn compact.

There is a not unimportant factor which should enter into a consideration of the amounts contributed by the two Provinces to which reference has been made. The Halifax Commission, sitting under the provisions of the Treaty of Washington, awarded Great Britain the sum of $5,500,000, to be paid by the United States for the privilege of using, for twelve years, the fisheries in the waters of Eastern Canada and upon the coast of Newfoundland. This amount was duly paid by the United States to the Imperial Government, who, thereupon, handed over to Newfoundland the sum of $1,000,000, as the share of that Island. Prince Edward Island, like Newfoundland, ratified the Treaty while a separate Province, and did not at the time of Confederation cede to Canada its right to compensation, and as the whole consensus of evidence before the Commission tended to prove that the fisheries on the coast of Prince Edward Island were the most valuable of any to which United States fishermen were admitted, the Island claimed the sum of $1,250,000 as its share, under the award. This demand, although frequently presented, the Dominion Government have steadily ignored, and have retained in the Federal Treasury the amount which the Island still claims as justly its right. The undersigned submit that, in any consideration of the contributions to the General Revenue, Prince Edward Island has a right to receive credit for the interest, at four per cent., upon the sum claimed, and which would amount annually to $50,000.

The undersigned cannot refrain from expressing their surprise that the Committee of Council, aware as they must have been, of the unequal circumstances of the two Provinces, should have adopted so unfair a comparison as that they propose now to review, and which is based upon partial and misleading returns. The positions of the two Provinces present no points of similarity. The figures quoted are for the year ended 30th June, 1884. At that time British Columbia possessed no direct means of communication with the settled portions of the Dominion at any season of the year, and accordingly was compelled to purchase almost all its supplies directly from other countries. These imports all paid duty at the ports of entry in British Columbia, and the amounts collected are credited to that Province. With Prince Edward Island, however, the circumstances are vastly different. Owing to its proximity to the older Provinces, a very large proportion (at least three-fourths) of the dutiable goods which its people use is purchased from wholesale houses in Quebec, Ontario, Nova Scotia, and New Brunswick. As will be readily understood, the duties upon these goods are collected at the ports of entry, and go to swell the apparent contributions of the other Provinces to the Dominion Exchequer. The Customs receipts, $171,443.89 (quoted by the Committee of Council at $170,863.40) represent only the duties upon the goods which the Island imports directly from countries outside of Canada, so that it is manifestly unfair, under such circumstances, to institute a comparison between British Columbia and Prince Edward Island. It is much to be regretted that the Dominion Government should labor under the grave misapprehension that the Customs duties collected in the ports of a Province can at all indicate its contributions to the general revenue. By a parity of reasoning, the metropolitan county of Middlesex, in Great Britain, might claim that it contributes the greater proportion of the Customs' revenues of the United Kingdom, while outlying or inland agricultural counties, such as Suffolk or Bucks, might be held as not yielding adequately to the Imperial Exchequer.

The difficulty of arriving at an absolutely correct calculation of the amount of dutiable goods which the people of Prince Edward Island consume cannot fail to be appreciated, yet the undersigned submit that there are several methods by which it may fairly be estimated. It must be premised that the people of the Island are very large consumers of dutiable goods for the reason that, being chiefly engaged in agriculture and fishing, their manufactures are very small as compared with the rest of

Canada, valuing, according to the last census returns, only $31.33 per head to $72.63 per head of the other Provinces.

In proof of the assertion that the people of the Island are principally engaged in agriculture and fishing, the undersigned would again advert to the Census Returns of 1881, which show that (the N. W. Territories not being included)—

One-half the area of Prince Edward Island is cultivated.

Only one-twenty-fifth of the other Provinces is cultivated.

Prince Edward Island has a population of 51 to the square mile.

The other Provinces only 4.72.

Prince Edward Island owns 55 animals of live stock for every 100 acres of improved land.

The other Provinces only 33.

In field products, Prince Edward Island raises to the acre of improved land 108¾ bushels.

The other Provinces only 61½ bushels.

From the Fisheries, Prince Edward Island produces $17.08 per head value.

The other Provinces $3.55.

The people of the Island are generally in comfortable circumstances, in proof of which may be adduced the amount of deposits per head in the Savings Banks, which averages $16.59 for the Island against $7.66 for the rest of the Dominion.

These figures clearly prove that the people of Prince Edward Island, from the fact of their not being extensive manufacturers, are under the necessity of using imported goods to a large extent, while the fertility of their soil, the value of their fisheries, and their general independence, demonstrate their ability to purchase. This being understood, the undersigned submit the following calculations, designed to show that the imports of dutiable goods into the Island are very much larger than suggested by the Committee of Council, and consequently the contributions to the Revenue peoportionately greater.

Method 1.

The average revenue of the Dominion from Customs and Excise, for the three years ended 30th June, 1884, was $27,603,479. The population of Prince Edward Island to that of the whole Dominion is in the proportion of 1 to 39.7. Upon this ratio, the Island's share of the Customs and Excise Revenue would amount to $695,301.

Method 2.

In 1872, the year before its admission into the Union, Prince Edward Island imported directly from countries beyond Canada, goods valued at..	$1,372,581	
The duty on which amounted to..		$184,227

And from Canada, goods the growth and manufacture of other countries, valued approximately at.................	429,354	
The duty on which amounted to.................		89,168
	$1,801,935	$273,395

It will surely not be argued that, in thirteen years, with a large increase in population, the Island's imports from countries outside the Dominion have decreased from $1,801,935 to $822,966, or over 45 per cent., yet this would appear to be the contention of the Committee of Council.

In 1861, the imports of the Island amounted to $1,021,669; in 1872, they had increased to $2,439,064, or at the rate of 138.9 per cent. At the same rate, its imports from countries beyond the Dominion should have increased from $1,801,935 in 1872 to $4,304,824 in 1884, which, at the present average tariff (free and dutiable combined) of 18.64 per cent., would give a customs Revenue of $802,419.

METHOD 3.

It is a well established principle that the imports and exports of a country bear a reasonable relation to each other. The imports of the Island for the ten years preceding Confederation aggregated in value £3,543,147 sterling. The exports in the same period, £2,559,091 sterling, showing that the imports exceeded the exports by about £100,000 sterling, or $500,000 annually. The imports of the Dominion for the last seventeen years aggregated in value $1,732,983,486; the exports in the same period, $1,390,946,803, showing that the imports exceeded the exports by about $20,000,000 annually, or in the same proportion, according to population, as the imports of Prince Edward Island exceeded the exports in the years already quoted.

The exports of the Island have steadily increased during the last 25 years. In 1861, it exported to all countries goods valued at $793,810, which had increased in 1872 to $1,497,058, or, at the rate of 88 3-5 per cent.

In 1872, the Island exported to countries beyond the Dominion goods valued at $722,333, which had increased in 1884 to $1,310,039, or at the rate of 81⅓ per cent.

Apply this rate of increase to the Island's imports from countries beyond the Dominion in 1872, and we have as a result for 1884, imports valued at $3,267,509.

But the figures, contained in the Dominion Trade and Navigation Returns, do not represent the total exports of the Island to countries beyond the Dominion, inasmuch as a considerable proportion, being shipped through Nova Scotia and New Brunswick territory, is credited to the exports of those Provinces. The annual export of horses from the Island to the United States is not less than 1,500, valued at $150,000. The Dominion returns for 1883-4 credit the Island with only 256, valued at

$27.486. This is but one instance of many. A considerable part of the large trade which the Island does in eggs with the United States, is credited to New Brunswick, while fish and potatoes, which are largely exported to Newfoundland, St. Pierre, and the West Indies, are much of them credited to Nova Scotia, being shipped by way of Halifax. In view of these facts, it would be within the mark to estimate, as indeed the Committee of Council admit, that the Island's Foreign Export Trade has doubled since 1872. Apply the same rate of increase to its imports from countries beyond the Dominion, as they stood in 1872, and we have as a result, for 1884, imports valued at $3,603,371, yielding, under an 18$\frac{64}{100}$ per cent. tariff, an annual revenue of $671,668.

The Exports of Prince Edward Island, since Confederation, have increased in a much larger ratio than have those of the Dominion, as the following figures will show:—

The total exports of the Dominion for 1871-2, were $82,639,683, for 1883-4, exclusive of the Island, $90,096,437, or an increase of only 9$\frac{1}{42}$ per cent., as against 100 per cent., by which the Island's exports have increased in the same time.

To recapitulate the results of the various methods:—

Method I.	$695,301
" II.	802,419
" III.	671,668
Average Annual Contribution by the Island from Customs and Excise	723,129
To which add Interest on the sum claimed as Island's share of Fishery Award (less amount expended for Fishing Bounties $8,569)	41,430
	$764,559

This sum of $764,559, the undersigned submit, should be accepted as closely approximating the annual contributions of Prince Edward Island to the Dominion Exchequer, and is much more likely to be within than in excess of the amount.

In proof of the assertion that a vast proportion of the dutiable goods which not only Prince Edward Island consumes, but Nova Scotia and New Brunswick as well, is imported from wholesale houses principally in the Province of Quebec, the undersigned present the following table, showing the amount per head apparently contributed to the Customs and Excise Revenues, in the following Provinces in 1881 and 1884, respectively:—

	1881.	1884.
Quebec	$7.29	$7.54
Ontario	4.78	5.14
New Brunswick	4.84	4.93
Nova Scotia	4.90	4.77
British Columbia	13.09	19.10
Prince Edward Island	2.76	1.78

It is absurd to suppose that the foregoing figures represent the actual consumption, per head, of dutiable goods, by the people of the various Provinces, rather do they prove that Quebec is the great importing and distributing Province for the whole of Eastern Canada. The extraordinary percentage for British Columbia is due, as the undersigned have already pointed out, to the peculiar circumstances of that Province in being compelled to import, almost exclusively, from countries beyond the Dominion, as well as to the inflation of trade, consequent upon the construction of the Canadian Pacific Railway and other large public works, no less than twelve millions of dollars having been expended thereon in 1885. Now that the Canadian Pacific Railway has been completed, it cannot be expected that the collections in British Columbia will be so large in the future, as they have been in the past. As has been the case with Prince Edward Island, so it will be in that Province. While the Canadian Pacific Railway will pour into British Columbia, British and West Indian goods, Quebec will continue to be the great importing and distributing Province, and in proportion as the Customs returns of British Columbia decrease, those of Quebec will increase.

The Committee of Council then proceeded to make a comparison as between British Columbia, Manitoba, the North-West Territories, and the Island, their figures being as follows:—

Total Revenue contributed by British Columbia, Manitoba, and the North-West Territories, $1,833,698.86, as against Prince Edward Island, $193,478.66.

The undersigned have only to remark that the same observations which they have applied to British Columbia, hold good in the case of Manitoba and the North-West Territories. No direct communication existed between those portions of the Dominion and the rest of Canada, when these returns were compiled, and consequently large imports of dutiable goods were made from the United States, with which country direct communication did exist. The immense inflation of trade consequent upon the construction, at so rapid a rate, of the Canadian Pacific Railway, upon which not less than 100 millions of dollars have been expended since 1881, accounts chiefly for the large returns from Manitoba and the North-West Territories, as well as from British Columbia.

The undersigned feel that no further arguments are necessary to prove that Prince Edward Island pays directly and indirectly into the Dominion Exchequer, Customs and Excise duties, at least four times as great as that stated by the Committee of Council, while, if the annual interest upon the amount claimed by the Island as its share of the Fishery Award be included, its contributions will be still further in excess of the sum estimated.

As evidence of the desire of the Dominion Government to promote the interests of Prince Edward Island, the Committee of Council submit a table of the expenditure upon the Island in the year 1884, amounting in the aggregate to $689,954.91.

Upon the first item, that of interest charged the Island on the Public Debt which the Dominion assumed, the undersigned observe that it is calculated at 5 per cent. As the whole amount of the Island Bonds, which the Dominion assumed at the time of Union, has been paid off, with the exception possibly of $1 000, the undersigned consider that it is unreasonable to charge the Island 5 per cent. on her proportion of the Public Debt, while the Dominion is able to borrow at 4 per cent., and while the latter is the average rate paid upon the aggregate debt of Canada. The difference between the two rates would cause a decrease in the amount charged of $39,081.51.

In like manner interest is charged 5 per cent. upon the capital expenditure on the Island Railway. Calculating the interest at 4 per cent., would reduce the sum by $5,789.20.

The undersigned observe also that the expense of operating the railway, in excess of the receipts, is charged at $91,924.01. They desire to remark that this amount includes the sum of $16,000 of extraordinary expenditure, which should not be debited to the Island, and they consider that it should be deducted.

The undersigned also observe that the subsidies to the steamers employed in the summer and winter service, and the men engaged in the Capes crossing, amounting to $32,876, are charged in full to the Island. This they consider unfair. Many of the inhabitants of the other Provinces derive equal advantages from this service with the people of the Island, and the means of communication provided are used to a much larger extent by the residents of the Mainland than by those of the Island. The undersigned therefore consider it only just that a portion of the expenditure thus incurred should be charged to Canada, and submit that not more than one-half of the sum expended in such connection should be debited to the Island, in which case an abatement would result of $16,438.

The subsidy to Fishwick's steamboat of $3,000 for communication between Halifax, Cape Breton and the Island, the undersigned submit, has no right to be charged in full to the Island; they object to more than one-third of the amount being so debited, and then a further reduction would be effected of $2,000.

These sums, which the undersigned consider should not in justice be charged to the Island, amount in the aggregate to $79,308.71, thus reducing the expenditure for 1884, as stated by the Committee of Council, to $610,646.20.

To recapitulate, the undersigned submit the following comparative statement of what the Island annually contributes to the General Revenue, and what it receives in return:—

Average annual contribution by the Island from Customs and Excise......		$723,129
To which add interest on the sum claimed by the Island as its share of the Fishery Award, less the sum paid for Fishing Bounties......................		41,430
		$764,559
Sum claimed by Committee of Council to be annually expended on the the Island..	$689,954	
Less amounts which undersigned contend should be deducted....	79,308	
		610,646
Excess of annual contributions of Prince Edward Island over Dominion expenditure..		$153,913

In proof of the efforts of the Dominion Government to provide improved means of communication, the Committee of Council adduce various items of *expenditure* since Confederation aggregating $951,698. Among these items appears the sum of $150,-000, appropriated for the construction of a pier at Cape Tormentine, *which has not been expended*, the site, so far as the undersigned are aware, not having yet been finally determined. Another item is that of $118,400, subsidy for the construction of a branch railway to Cape Tormentine. This road is only about half completed, and the subsidy *paid* up to November last, when the Report of the Committee of Council was adopted, did not exceed $20,000. Neither do the undersigned consider that the whole of this subsidy should be charged against the Island. The work is situate in the Province of New Brunswick, and must be presumed to be of great benefit thereto, otherwise a private Company would not undertake to build it without any previous assurance of assistance from the Federal Government. Besides, the subsidy has only been granted in accordance with a policy pursued by the Dominion Government of giving aid to certain lines of railway on the mainland. The sum of $12,400, to pay the Island Government for a pier at Cape Traverse, is also included in the *expenditure*, though at the time the Committee of Council made their Report that amount had not been *paid.* Another item is for cable service, which doubtless means the subsidy of £400 sterling annually paid to the Anglo-American Telegraph Company. As the assumption of this subsidy by the General Government was under a distinct and separate article of the Terms of Confederation, and has no connection with communication by steam across the Straits, the undersigned object to its being included in the expenditure for the improvement of steam communication. This subsidy for twelve years amounts to $23,372. The Committee of Council include also in their memorandum the subsidies for the summer mail service and for the winter crossing at the Capes. As similar amounts were paid by the Island Government previous to Confederation, and as they represent only the cost of maintaining the communication which the Island had before the Union, the undersigned cannot admit that they should be included as expenditure for *improving* the means of communication.

The undersigned consider that these various items to which they have taken objection should be deducted from the amount which the Committee of Council claim to have been expended, when the memorandum of expenditure would read as follows:—

Amount claimed to have been expended		$951,698
Deduct for Cape Tormentine Pier, not expended	$150,000	
Allow one-half paid as subsidy to Cape Tormentine Branch Railway and deduct balance	108,400	
Deduct half of Summer Mail and Iceboat Service	196,073	
Deduct for Cape Traverse Pier	12,400	
Deduct Cable Service	23,372	
		$490,245
Leaving		$461,453

as the amount *actually expended* within the last 12 years to meet the wishes of the Island and to give improved means of communication with the mainland.

In the foregoing pages the undersigned have endeavored to show and, as they consider, have clearly established—

(1) That the Dominion Government voluntarily, and without any solicitation on the part of the Island, covenanted to provide continuous communication, by efficient steam service, winter and summer, between the Island and the mainland—that this engagement they have entirely failed to carry out. Further, that the Dominion Government have never, up to the present winter, provided in any manner, for the transport of passengers when obliged to resort to the Capes' route, where they have not even attempted the use of steamers, that they have failed to carry out the promises made by their ministers to the representatives of the Island, and, generally, that they have displayed great inactivity and reluctance to improve such communication as has been afforded.

(2) That the Committee of Council have erred in representing that the Domin-

ion expenditures exceed, by more than three times, the amount received from the Island; the undersigned having plainly demonstrated, as they believe, that the Island contributes to the Dominion Exchequer an amount far in excess of what is expended.

(3) That the amount which the Committee of Council claim to have been expended by the Dominion Government in the improvement of the means of communication with the mainland is largely in excess of the sum actually paid therefor.

Referring to other points, the Committee of Council state that "since the Union, a subsidy of $10,000 a year has been paid by the Dominion Government to the Prince Edward Island Steam Navigation Company, to run steamers daily during the season of open navigation, from Shediac in New Brunswick to Summerside on the Island, and from Pictou in Nova Scotia to Charlottetown and Georgetown." The undersigned desire to correct a misapprehension under which the Committee of Council seem to labor, that daily communication exists between Nova Scotia and the Island. This is not the case, as the steamers connect with Pictou only four times a week. Lest it might be inferred that the payment of $10,000 a year for this service was under a recent agreement entered into by the Dominion Government with the Steam Navigation Company, the undersigned desire to say that such agreement was made by the Island Government previous to Confederation, and the Dominion, in now paying that amount, is only carrying out that agreement.

The statement of the Committee of Council that "previous to the Union, paddle-wheel steamers were employed," might lead to the supposition that since then the Dominion Government have obtained the substitution of screw-steamers. The undersigned desire to say that the identical boats which plied on the route for nearly ten years previous to the Union are still the only ones employed in that service.

Adverting to the Report of the Committee of Parliament in 1883, upon the best means of improving the communication between the Island and the mainland, the undersigned find that many recommendations were made upon which they desire to offer some remarks.

That Committee recommended that the crossing at the Capes should be undertaken by the Government, rather than let by contract, yet this suggestion was not acted upon until the present winter.

In regard to the Iceboat Service at the Capes, the Committee of Parliament recommended that stations for observation and Signal Service should be adopted for the guidance of the boats while crossing. No such stations have been provided.

The Committee of Parliament also stated it as their opinion, from the evidence before them, that a small screw-steamer could be used during a considerable portion of the winter in connection with the iceboats, and could be safely docked in the board-ice when not at work, and they recommended the Government to take measures to test, by actual experiment, the feasibility of this project. No such steamer has been provided, nor has any attempt been made to test the practicability of such a project.

The Committe of Parliament further reported that the boats of the Steam Navigation Company, subsidized by the Dominion Government, were altogether inadequate to perform the work required of them; that, being driven by paddle-wheels, they are not capable of contending with ice, and that suitable screw-boats could continue crossing about three weeks later in the fall, and commence two or three weeks earlier in the spring, and they recommended that good substantial boats should be provided to meet the requirements of the Island, and that at least one of these boats should be a screw-boat, of such construction as would enable her to run as late in the fall, and as early in the spring as a proper regard for the safety of life and property would permit.

This recommendation has been wholly disregarded, and, notwithstanding the fact that the contract with the Steam Navigation Company expired two years ago, the same paddle-wheel boats, which have been engaged in the service for the last twenty-two years, are still employed.

The Committee of Parliament further recommended that, inasmuch as the evidence taken before them went to show that the *Northern Light* was fast becoming unfit for service, another suitable steamer should be provided to take her place.

This recommendation has also been disregarded, the *Northern Light* being still employed, and although she annually undergoes some repairs, her seaworthiness is open to grave question.

The undersigned have thus deemed it necessary to call attention, at considerable length, to the indifference shown by the Dominion Government to the recommendations of a Committee of Parliament who, the Committee of Council state, reached their conclusions "after long and careful consideration of the subject, and examination of persons, papers and records."

The Committee of Council say that "the change from sailing vessels to steamers, for summer, appears to have been the only improvement effected by the Island Government, in their means of communication in fifty years, although having control of a larger sum in revenue than the Island now pays into the Dominion." The unfairness of the latter part of this statement, the undersigned having already pointed out they need not again refer to it. They would merely remark, that the promise to overcome the obstructions which, for so large a portion of the year, had cut the people of the Island off from connection with the mainland, was one of the principal inducements for them to enter the Union, and they considered that, by confederating with Canada, the co-operation of many of the people of the other Provinces, who were interested equally with the people of the Island, would be secured.

The Committee of Council state that, during the last two seasons, the average number of passengers in each crossing of the *Northern Light*, was only a fraction over nine. While not disputing the correctness of this calculation, it is instructive to note that, about three years ago, an order was issued by the Department of Marine, restricting the number of passengers upon any trip to thirty. The making of such an order, the undersigned submit, is sufficient proof that, at times, the passenger travel is large; indeed, the steamer has occasionally carried from 80 to 100 persons. It may be remarked that the officers of the *Northern Light* have found it impossible to enforce the order restricting the number of passengers to 30, and that it has remained inoperative almost ever since its promulgation.

On this point the undersigned desire to introduce an extract from a speech delivered last session, in the Senate, by the Hon. Mr. Haythorne, wherein he called attention to the very large number of passengers crossing at times in the *Northern Light*, and to the want of accommodation afforded by that steamer. He spoke as follows:—

"On my return home from my duties in this House last spring, I was detained on the mainland for two or three days awaiting a change of weather, which would enable the *Northern Light* to come to Pictou. A telegram informed us that she had left Georgetown on her passage. Ultimately she arrived, bringing, as it was said, about 100 passengers. The point to which I wish to draw the attention of the House, and particularly the attention of the Government, is, that there were from 75 to 87 passengers on board on her return; my honorable friend who sits opposite (Mr. Montgomery) says there were 87 passengers on board, but this I have no hesitation in saying there was barely standing room, to say nothing of sitting accommodation, which one expects to find in a passenger steamer. Hon gentlemen might suppose that there was a simple remedy for this, by instructing the captain not to take more than a certain number of passengers on board. Well, that of course would be a remedy, but it would be a vast inconvenience, and it would be something more; it would be a cruel thing, because it is within my knowledge that, last spring, numbers of poor people were waiting for a passage across, and they had not the means to pay their expenses, if they had been long detained there. I was informed that some of them went out and sought work, while waiting for the arrival of the *Northern Light;* and therefore, while taking fewer passengers might be a remedy for the danger, it would be cruel, when the Government have another vessel, fully capable of assisting the *Northern Light*, to detain passengers there."

The Committee of Council state that the small passenger list of the *Northern Light*, and the large annual deficit in working the Island Railway, are the best evidence of the limited travel to be provided for. The undersigned submit that this argument constitutes no justification for the failure of the Dominion Government to carry out their obligations to the Island. So long as Communication with the Mainland is at all certain, the traffic is large, but with the irregular movements of the "Northern Light," and the doubt that exists as to her seaworthiness, it is not extraordinary that travel and traffic are limited. So far as the Island Railway is concerned, traffic is restricted, for the reason that, after the close of navigation, no shipments can be made from the Island. Were the Island's communication with the Intercolonial Railway and the other railways of the Dominion continuous, as Canada solemnly promised it should be, the case would be different.

The Committee of Council desire it to be borne in mind that the Dominion Government did not undertake the carrying of agricultural produce nor freight of any kind. although they have at all times afforded facility for the transport of any freight offering, The facility afforded may be judged of when it is explained that the freight capacity of the "Northern Light" is not more than 200 barrels. But while it is true that the Dominion Government did not expressly undertake the carrying of freight, it is well known that freight traffic is more remunerative than passenger traffic, and that if a larger and more powerful steamer had been provided, having increased cargo room, the returns would have been much greater, and the outlay proportionally less.

The Committee of Council say that "it will be claimed on behalf of the Island that the population consumes goods the produce of the Mainland, but that, while this is true, the same occurred previous to the Confederation;" and they proceed to quote the value of the imports of the Island from the Dominion in 1872, upon which duties were collected, at $1,067,480. The undersigned desire to say that this amount accurately represents the value of the Island's imports in 1872 from and through the Dominion of Canada, but that in those imports there were included dutiable goods the growth and manufacture of other countries valued at $371,163, as also articles on which the Island levied no duty, valued at $58,190; so that, these amounts being deducted, the sum of $638,127 would represent the real value of our imports from the Dominion.

The Committee of Council state that the total value of goods entered for consumption in Prince Edward Island from all countries, in 1872, was $1,605,241. The undersigned cannot conceive where such information was obtained. They have carefully examined the Trade Returns of the Island for that year, and they find the total Imports into the Island amounted in value to $2,439,078, nearly if not all of which were entered for Home Consumption. The undersigned must express their regret that so grave a misapprehension should be entertained by the Committee of Council as to the trade of the Island.

The Committee of Council say that "no doubt the same interprovincial trade continues with this change in favor of Prince Edward Island—that the goods from the other Provinces are now free of duty, whilst, previous to the Union, they paid duties the same as on importations from other countries." There can be no doubt that interprovincial trade continues, as the present tariff of the Dominion is framed with the special view of encouraging manufactures. This trade is, however, much more advantageous to the other Provinces than to the Island, as it is impossible that manufactures can be carried on, on the Island, to any great extent while regular communication with the mainland is interrupted for over four months of the year. That the people of the Island obtain certain goods from the other Provinces free of duty is true, but the statement is, nevertheless, misleading. Protected by a high Customs duty, the Quebec or Ontario manufacturer is able to obtain in many lines of goods, prices nearly, if not altogether, equal to the cost and duty of the same goods of British or Foreign manufacture. Situated as Canada is, and having a view to the infant state of her manufactures, and the tariff policy of the United States, the undersigned believe the fiscal policy of Canada to be a justifiable one; but while the Terms of Union in the matter of Steam Communication remain unfulfilled, the people of the Island are precluded, to a considerable extent, from participating in the benefits which that policy is calculated to confer.

The Committee of Council, while admitting that the Island may have felt inconvenience from the interruption in the trips of the *Northern Light*, yet consider that the material interests of the Province have not greatly suffered, owing to the fact that its exports to foreign countries have nearly doubled from 1872 to 1884. The undersigned fail to comprehend why this argument should be admitted in justification of the failure of the Dominion Government to carry out the Terms of Union. That the Island has improved, is notwithstanding the inaction of the Dominion Government, and its progress is due to its natural resources and the great industry of its people, and tends to show how much greater its prosperity would have been had it enjoyed the continuous communication which was guaranteed it, and which it had a right to expect. The Island's contributions to the Federal Treasury in excess of the expenditure, together with the money which has been uselessly expended upon the inefficient communication afforded, would very probably be adequate to defray the interest upon a sum necessary to construct a work which would effectually overcome its isolation. Here the undersigned desire to say that the Ministry of Prince Edward Island, so far from regarding the Canadian Pacific Railway as a local work for the benefit of British Columbia only (as alleged by the Committe of Council), have always warmly supported the present Administration of the Dominion in their policy of constructing that great national highway; and all that they now ask is that a work of vast importance, not only to the Island but to the whole of the Dominion, as solemnly guaranteed as was the Railway to British Columbia, should be undertaken and brought to a successful completion.

Within the past few months a scheme has been proposed which, it is claimed, will successfully remove the disabilities from which the Island has so long suffered. Engineers of the highest standing in America, and whose reputations are well established in Great Britain, have given it as their opinion that it is practicable to lay a metallic subway across the Straits of Northumberland, through which railway communication could be effected, and that the cost of such an undertaking would not exceed a sum which it would not be unreasonable to ask the Government of Canada to expend. During the past summer, soundings were taken, and the bed of the Straits was found to be admirably adapted for the laying of the tube, the Admiralty charts corroborating the results of the examination which was made.

The Committee of Council speak of the "liberal treatment" of the Island by the Dominion Government, and that it has received especial consideration, on account of its isolated position, though possessing a population less than some cities on the Mainland. To this statement the undersigned desire to except. They have clearly proved, as they believe, that Prince Edward Island contributes to the genera revenue, more than is returned in expenditure. To the unfortunate misapprehension that the Island is being treated with exceptional liberality, and that it does not return to the general revenue one-third of the amount expended, is probably due the invidious distinction made by the General Government in the remuneration of their officials on the Island. The same erroneous impression has possibly influenced the General Government in declining, up to the present time, to maintain many of the public piers in the Province, although expressly bound to do so by the British North America Act.

The Committee of Council say "the 'Northern Light' was placed at Charlottetown as head quarters; her officers and crew are inhabitants of the Island, and her unceasing and hazardous efforts to make communication in the severest weather cannot be unknown to the Island Government." The Committee of Council seem to entertain the idea that the officers and crew of the "Northern Light," being Island men, are consequently bold enthusiasts, and would be willing to incur great risk in the effort to maintain communication with the Mainland. The undersigned desire to remark that, whatever zeal the officers of the "Northern Light" have displayed in the performance of their duties, their ardor must have been considerably dampened by the instructions which were issued some time ago by the Department of Marine, and which are as follow:—

"OTTAWA, Jan. 16, 1883.

"Capt. Finlayson, steamer *Northern Light*.

"Telegram received urging Department order you run. Responsibility is with you. Expect you to run no undue risks.

"A. W. MCLELAN."

Two days later, on receipt of a telegram from Capt. Finlayson asking instructions, the following was sent him:—

"OTTAWA, Jan. 18, 1883.

"Capt. Finlayson, steamer *Northern Light*.

"With knowledge of ice, you must be judge, and held responsible for safety of boat. Incur no undue risks.

"WM. SMITH."

"SIR,— "OTTAWA, Jan. 12, 1884.

"Referring to my letter of 14th December, 1882, I have again to instruct you to use your own judgment as to whether the *Northern Light* should run, and you are to incur no risk whereby the safety of the vessel may be endangered by being caught in the ice. No risk also is to be incurred for the purpose of carrying over any particular passenger or passengers, and the Department expects that you will use your judgment in all matters affecting the running of the boat, and will hold you responsible for her safety.

"Capt. A. Finlayson, WM. SMITH,
" *Northern Light.* Deputy Minister of Marine."

The undersigned submit that these instructions were quite sufficient to discourage and deter the officers of the *Northern Light* from making those strenuous efforts to effect a crossing which otherwise they might have been disposed to do.

Under the British North America Act, and the terms agreed upon subsequently, with the various Provinces, Canada undertook to effect the following great public works, with the object of connecting, by the bonds of commercial relationship, the political union which had been entered into, viz: The Canadian Pacific Railway, the Intercolonial Railway, the deepening and widening of the great Canals, and Communication by Steam, Winter and Summer, with Prince Edward Island. The first three of these undertakings have been carried out with the cordial concurrence and support of the people of Prince Edward Island. The sum of about $43,000,000, a much larger amount than was anticipated, has been spent on the Intercolonial Railway, and although that road has not yet paid more than working expenses, the General Government have granted large subsidies to a competing line of Railway The people of Prince Edward Island are very far from objecting to the faith of the country being maintained inviolate, and to liberal expenditure being made for necessary public works, and have cheerfully borne their share of the burdens, but they do complain that the communication guaranteed them by the Terms of Confederation, is not provided, although the expenditure necessary to do so would be very small compared with the enormous outlay incurred on the other public works to which the undersigned have referred.

With regard to the claim for compensation by reason of the non fulfilment of the Terms of Confederation, the undersigned submit that a review of the facts adduced will conclusively show that the Island has suffered great loss, and is therefore entitled to indemnity. Should further evidence on this point be needed, the undersigned will be pleased to supply the same, as well as to furnish any other information that may be required by your Lordship in order to a full consideration of the whole case.

We have the honor to be,

Your Lordship's most obedient humble Servants,

W. W. SULLIVAN,
D. FERGUSON.

THE RIGHT HONORABLE EARL GRANVILLE, K. G.
Secretary of State for the Colonies

COLONIAL OFFICE,
Downing Street, 9th March, 1886.

GENTLEMEN,—

I am directed by Earl Granville to acknowledge the receipt of your letter of the 1st instant, relative to the question of the establishment of Steam Communication between Prince Edward Island and the mainland.

I am to state that His Lordship would be glad if it should suit your convenience to meet him at his office on Friday next at 3 p. m. His Lordship has invited Sir Charles Tupper to attend for the purpose of informally discussing the matter referred to in your letter.

I am, Gentlemen,

Your obedient Servant,

(Signed) ROBERT G. W. HERBERT.

W. W. SULLIVAN, Esq.,
D. FERGUSON, Esq.

PRINCE EDWARD ISLAND.

Memorandum by Sir Charles Tupper on the Observations submitted by the Prince Edward Island Delegates to Earl Granville in their Paper of March 1, 1886.

THE rejoinder, addressed to Earl Granville, of the Prince Edward Island Delegates—Messrs. Sullivan and Ferguson—to the Report of the Committee of the Privy Council of Canada respecting the Memorial to Her Majesty on the subject of the communication between the island and the mainland, commences by a general justification of the memorial in question,

They then quote from the Report of the Committee of the Privy Council—Messrs. McLelan and Campbell—"that it is altogether improbable that any man who had seen the straits of Northumberland, or had any knowledge of ice obstruction in mid-winter, could have supposed it possible to construct a steamer capable of crossing when the ice is at its heaviest in that season." They do not, however, comment upon this statement, or deny it, but content themselves by remarking that the offer of continuous steam communication, summer and winter, was entirely a voluntary act on the part of the Dominion, and they submit that it should be carried out. They do not contend that it is practicable to do so, but merely repeat the language of the memorial to Her Majesty that "no sufficient disposition has been shown by the Dominion Government to fulfil their obligations towards the Island in this matter." Then they state the failure of the first vessel employed in 1874 and 1875, the "Albert." The unsuitability of the "Northern Light," put on the service in 1876, is also commented upon, and it is added that "she was not specially designed for the service." The report of Messrs. McLelan and Campbell gives a clear answer to the allegations so far mentioned. In the first place they point out, very fairly, that prior to Confederation there was a regular service during the summer season, but that for five months or more, during the latter part of the autumn, the winter and the early spring, there was no steam service at all, the mails—and presumably passengers—being carried by ice-boats from Cape Traverse to Cape Tormentine, and thence by sleigh to Amherst, the land carriage being 52 miles, and the distance from Cape to Cape 9 miles. This appears to demonstrate very clearly that the Island Government had not found "continuous steam service" practicable during the winter season, otherwise the assumption is that they would have adopted it before Confederation. But they appear to imagine that all the difficulties which to them had been insurmountable, should have entirely vanished when the Island joined the Dominion. In the circumstances the phrase "continuous steam service" might fairly and properly have been accepted with the qualification "as far as practicable," and the obligations have been carried out by the Dominion Government in this spirit. The impossibility of continuous steam communication in mid-winter has been fully demonstrated, as pointed out by Messrs. McLelan and Campbell, but the efforts of the Dominion have been so far successful as to reduce the period of interruption to an average of one-third of what it was previous to the Union. Messrs. Sullivan and Ferguson say that the "Northern Light" is not suitable for the service, and was not specially designed for the work. They apparently forget that in the joint address to the Governor-General from the Legislative Council and House of Assembly, in 1881, this same vessel is spoken of as having been "constructed expressly for the work and placed upon the route," although complaint was made of the irregular and unsatisfactory trips she made. Upon this point Messrs. McLelan and Campbell say:—"The Dominion Government, after a most careful and anxious inquiry, contracted with a Mr. Sewell of Quebec, to complete a powerful steamer on a model specially designed for ice service. In December, 1876, this steamer, named the "Northern Light" was completed and placed upon the route between Pictou and Charlottetown, and has been maintained each winter to date at an aggregate cost, including construction, of $249,956.57."

No representation appears to have been made in the matter to the Dominion Government until 1881, although the "Northern Light" was put on in 1876. Messrs. Sullivan and Ferguson state the average period the vessel is unavailable during the winter as 70 days; in the address to Her Majesty 64 days is given and the Parliamentary Committee at Ottawa in 1883 gave 48 days as the average. The latter also said in their report that "the daily records kept by the captain of the "Northern Light" and the testimony given by the officers show that the heavy ice encountered was the cause that compelled him to discontinue crossing in mid-winter;" and, further, that "the evidence of the officers examined is also to the effect that the steamer is not sufficient to overcome the difficulties of the winter navigation, and although they suggest slight improvements on her model, which would better fit her for the purposes for which she was intended, still are unanimously of opinion that no steamship can be built capable of keeping up continuous communication in mid-winter between the island and the mainland." They add, "we examined personally several gentlemen of large practical experience in crossing from the island in winter season, all of whom confirm the above, and whose evidence is hereto appended." This Committee consisted of three representatives from Prince Edward Island, and two from the mainland, and surely their opinions are worthy of credence, and justify the contention of the Dominion Government that the utmost has been done to carry out the terms under which the Island entered the Union. Messrs. McLelan and Campbell in their report also say, "If continuous steam communication has not been maintained, it is certainly not because the Dominion Government sought to avoid expense. The "Northern Light" is as large and as powerful a steamer as experience in Arctic exploration has proved advisable, and she is kept on full expense, equipped and ready to run at all times during the entire winter, and, were it possible to do so, no additional expense would be incurred, except for fuel, whilst the cost of the ice-boat service would be saved. and the construction of railways, piers, and boat-houses to and at Capes Traverse and Tormentine, rendered unnecessary." The Government have, it may be added, spent, or are committed to spend, about $951,698 in connection with the communication between Prince Edward Island and the mainland.

The remainder of the rejoinder addressed to Lord Granville refers to other matters, some of which do not directly refer to the questions at issue.

Messrs. Sullivan and Ferguson call attention to the speech of Sir Alexander Campbell in the Senate in 1884, respecting the provision of one of the lighthouse steamers to supplement the "Northern Lightt" during the winter, which certainly seems to have been promised. Considering the narrowness of the Strait, it appears doubtful if a second steamer would be of much advantage, but in any case there is no mention of the matter in the papers in the possession of the High Commissioner for Canada.

They admit, as Messrs. McLelan and Campbell contended, that a railway to Cape Traverse had been built and a pier constructed, although stating that the latter requires some alterations; also that the railway to Cape Tormentine is being made with the aid of a large subsidy from the Dominion Government. Complaint is made that although an appropriation has been made for a pier at Cape Tormentine, its construction has not yet been commenced. But the Dominion Government have said that it will be built, and no doubt the delay is owing to the time taken in laying the railway, with which it will be connected.

Messrs. Sullivan and Ferguson combat the statement of Messrs. McLelan and Campbell, that the Island Government were fully conversant with the whole action and plans of the Dominion Government, and raise a question respecting the erection of boat-houses, in which some delay occurred. The boat houses were, however, finished last year, and the criticism mentioned, therefore, seems in this view to be rather captious, especially as nothing is said in the same paragraph about the railway and pier at Cape Traverse, and the railway to and the pier at Cape Tormentine which the Government have warmly taken up, and of which it must be presumed the Island Government were fully informed.

It is stated also by Messrs. Sullivan and Ferguson that "the Dominion Government have totally neglected, ever since Confederation, to make any provision whatever for the transport of passengers when compelled to resort to the Capes route." In explanation of this may be quoted an extract from a letter that has recently been received from Mr. McLelan, the late Minister of Marine and Fisheries of Canada. "The *Northern Light* made regular trips this season until the 27th January, or some time last week. I took (as Minister of Marine and Fisheries), charge of the crossing at the Capes, and there is now a good organization and equipment The delegates crossed by that route, and I believe they said it was the first time that they had ever been brought over—that is, they had on all previous occasions to work their passage."

Messrs. McLelan and Campbell, in referring to the Parliamentary Committee of 1883, state: "It is the unanimous opinion of members of the Committee, confirmed by the testimony of witnesses of large practical experience, that no steamships can be built capable of keeping up continuous communication in mid-winter." Messrs. Sullivan and Ferguson say: "The undersigned have examined the report of the said Parliamentary Committee, and have failed to discover therein that they came to this conclusion." This may be literally correct, but the actual wording of the report quoted below of the Committee shows that Messrs. McLelan and Campbell had every foundation for making the statement "The evidence of the officers examined is also to the effect that the steamer is not sufficient to overcome the difficulties of the winter navigation, and although they suggest slight improvements on her model, which would better fit her for the purposes for which she was intended, still are unanimously of opinion that no steamship can be built capable of keeping up continuous communication in mid-winter between the Island and the Mainland." "We examined personally several gentlemen of large practical experience in crossing from the Island in the winter season, all of whom confirm the above, and whose evidence is hereto appended."

Messrs. Sullivan and Ferguson in their rejoinder deprecate the action of Messrs. McLelan and Campbell in comparing the amounts contributed to the revenue by British Columbia and Prince Edward Island respectively. But they should remember that the controversy was started in the memorial to Her Majesty by drawing attention to the treatment the former Province was said to have received by the rapid construction of the Canadian Pacific Railway, although its population of white people was comparatively small. It would have been far better had the special question at issue been dealt with upon its merits; but for the departure from this sound principle the Dominion Government cannot be blamed.

Messrs. Sullivan and Ferguson dispute altogether the accuracy of the proportion of the revenue of the Dominion contributed by the Island, as specified by Messrs. McLelan and Campbell, but before going into details they remark that in any such calculations interest should be allowed on $1,250,000, the proportion of the Halifax Fishery Award claimed by the Island, which they say would annually amount to $50,000. It must be remembered, in the first place, that the position in this matter of Prince Edward Island is precisely the same as that of Nova Scotia and New Brunswick, and different to that of Newfoundland, which has not joined the Confederation, and is therefore a separate Colony. Prince Edward Island has been treated similarly to the other Maritime Provinces in every respect, and has shared in the general benefit derived from the measures taken by the Government in connection with the fisheries, and has participated in the payments of bounties to fishermen. Messrs. Sullivan and Ferguson do not appear to be aware also that prior to Prince Edward Island joining the Confederation, the Island made arrangements with the United States in regard to the inshore fisheries differing from those made by Canada. In fact they allowed the United States fishermen to share the inshore fisheries on the unratified understanding that the exports of fish to the United States should not be charged duty, or in any case that any duty charged should be refunded. When the American Government refused to ratify these arrangements, the Dominion Government refunded the duties to Prince Edward Island, and this should be taken into consideration in connection with the matter.

The long discussion entered into by Messrs. Sullivan and Ferguson with the object of showing that the revenue contributed by the Island to the Dominion, as stated in the Trade and Navigation Returns, is incorrect, and gives an inaccurate idea of the actual position of the Island in this respect, opens up an interminable source of argument. Messrs. McLelan and Campbell quote this revenue as $193,474, as against $942,095 in British Columbia, and $891,683 in Manitoba and the North-West. Messrs. Sullivan and Ferguson base their objections to the figures on the ground that the Island's imports, upon which the revenue is collected, come from countries outside Canada, and that since Confederation a very large portion of the articles consumed come from the maritime provinces and Quebec and Ontario, having already paid duty in those provinces, which should in any revenue calculations be credited to the island. They proceed to make hypothetical estimates of the actual imports and of the actual revenue on various bases, assuming the importations had been made direct, and chargeable at an average duty of 18.64 per cent. By these methods they bring up the revenue contributed by the island to $764,559 as the average of three calculations. Then the larger figures of

British Columbia and Manitoba and the North-west territories are accounted for by stating that at that time (1884) British Columbia possessed no direct means of communication with the settled portions of the Dominion, at any season of the year, and accordingly was compelled to purchase almost all its supplies directly from other countries. These imports all paid duties at the ports of entry in British Columbia, and the amounts collected are credited to that province. The same reasons, they allege, also apply to Manitoba and the North-west territories. This does not seem to bear upon the question of "continuous steam service." It cannot, however, be too often stated, that the communication between the island and the mainland has been more regular in winter since 1873, than before Confederation, and that the period of interruption is now not more than one-third of what it was, and that a regular daily steam service is an impossibility, as evidenced by the report of the Parliamentary Committee which in 1883 enquired into the matter. But apart from this, the reasons advanced by Prince Edward Island to account for its small revenue apply to every province, more or less, as there is a large general inter-provincial trade, and as the island admittedly participates in such trade it must be presumed that the inhabitants of the province find it to their advantage to do so rather than to get their imports from other sources.

The amount spent annually in Prince Edward Island (in 1884 it was $689,954, although this is disputed also), demonstrates the way in which the island has been treated by the Dominion Government, and upon this point Messrs. McLelan and Campbell say, "The liberal treatment of Prince Edward Island results from the policy and practice of the Dominion Government to watch over the interests of the smaller provinces, and Prince Edward Island from her isolated position, and with a population less than some cities on the mainland, has received especial consideration." Messrs. Sullivan and Ferguson admit that the exports from the island to countries beyond the Dominion in 1884 were 81⅓ per cent. more than they were in 1872, and that the amount per head deposited in the savings' banks averages $16·59 as against $7·66 for the rest of the Dominion. This does not indicate that much injury has resulted to the island from the want of continuous steam service, and clearly proves the benefit derived from the connection of the island with the Confederation, and the improved service since 1873. The total customs revenue of the island in 1872 was about $302,000, and admitting for the sake of argument, that it amounts to $764,559 now, this increase of 120 per cent. does not support their case that injury has resulted to the island from the terms of the Union not having been fulfilled, and that it has obtained no advantage from joining the Dominion, and from the encouragement that has been given to inter-provincial trade and manufacturing industry.

Messrs. Sullivan and Ferguson also object to the figures given by Messrs. McLelan and Campbell as representing the expenditure upon the island in 1884. The amount specified is $689,954, but they contend that $79,308 should be deducted. The total they admit, however, is $610,646 and the difference relates to controversial matters.

Messrs. Sullivan and Ferguson say "The statement of the Committee of Council that, previous to the Union, paddle-wheel steamers were employed, might lead to the supposition that since then the Dominion Government have obtained the substitution of screw steamers, but the undersigned desire to say that the identical boats which plied on the route for nearly ten years previous to the Union are still the only ones employed in the service." What Messrs. McLelan and Campbell did say was—"Previous to the Union, paddle-wheel steamers only were employed, and it was very generally believed, and for good reasons, that a screw steamer would maintain steam communication to a much later period, but it is altogether improbable that any man who had seen the Straits of Northumberland or had any knowledge of the ice obstruction in mid-winter could have supposed it possible to construct a steamer capable of crossing when the ice is at its heaviest, in that season, and it is proper to assume that both contracting parties to the Union having such knowledge understood that the Dominion Government would provide and maintain the means which science and experience might determine as the best and most efficient for the end in view, within the range of possibility." This full extract places a different light upon the matter, and it has been amply demonstrated above that the Dominion Government has done its best to provide continuous steam service "within the range of possibility," and that its efforts have been beneficial to the island.

Objection is also taken to the remark of the Committee of Council, "that the change from sailing vessels to steamers, for summer, appears to have been the only improvement effected by the Island Government in their means of communication in fifty years, although having control of a larger sum in revenue than the island now pays the Dominion." The first part is not denied by Messrs. Sullivan and Ferguson, but the revenue question is again disputed. They go on to say that the prospect of continuous steam service was one of the principal inducements that led the island to enter the Dominion. Messrs. McLelan and Campbell's report gives the impression that they desired to convey the idea that although the Island Government had not done much, before Confederation to provide continuous steam service in winter, the Dominion Government had since that time much improved the communication, and this cannot be denied.

The next point of difference is the number of passengers using this route. Messrs. McLelan and Campbell say that during the past two winter seasons the average number of passengers in each crossing of the *Northern Light* was only nine (the average of the present season so far is said to have been only six); also that the loss on the Island Railway since its opening has been $843,911, besides an expenditure thereon on capital account of about $500,000. Messrs. Sullivan and Ferguson, in reply, give instances of 100 passengers crossing at one time. This only proves how small the number must have been on other occasions, if the average of each crossing is only nine. Then they say that the number of passengers would be greater if the service were more regular, *and the seaworthiness of the ship more assured.* This latter is a grave charge against the Dominion Government, and cannot be allowed to pass without protest, especially as the statement is but a general one and unsubstantiated.

Exception is also made to the remark of the Committee of Council, "that the Dominion Government did not undertake the carrying of agricultural produce or freight of any kind, although they have at all times afforded facility for the transport of any offering." Messrs. Sullivan and Ferguson say, "The facility afforded may be judged of when it is explained that the freight capacity of the *Northern Light* is not more than two hundred barrels." It must be remembered that the phrase "continuous steam service" applied to passengers and mails only, and *any* provision for freight is therefore a gain to the province.

Messrs. McLelan and Campbell say, "It will be claimed on behalf of the island that the population consumes goods the produce of the mainland. No doubt this is true, but the same occurred previous to the confederation." The figures for 1872 are given as $1,067,480. The Prince Edward Island delegates state that of this $371,163 came from countries other than Canada, although through Dominion ports, reducing the imports from Canada to $638,127. The accuracy of these figures (there is no means of checking them in the office of the High Commissioner), does not affect the general question.

The Dominion Government gave the total value of the goods entered for consumption in the island in 1872 as $1,605,241. This Messrs. Sullivan and Ferguson object to, and state that the figures should be $2,439,078. There are no means of checking this in the office of the High Commissioner.

Messrs. McLelan and Campbell say that "No doubt the same inter-provincial trade continues with this change in favour of Prince Edward Island—that the goods from the other provinces are now free of duty, whilst previous to the Union they paid duties the same as on importations from other countries." Messrs. Sullivan and Ferguson do not object to this, and express their concurrence in the present fiscal policy of Canada; but they say that the existing tariff is more favorable to other provinces than to the island, as the latter has no manufactures, and that the Quebec and Ontario manufacturers "protected by a high customs' duty" are able to obtain in many lines of goods prices nearly if not altogether equal to the cost and duty of the same goods of British or foreign manufacture. This sounds rather paradoxical, but it is evident from the increased prosperity of the island; from its increased exports, and from its increased savings bank deposits, that no injury has resulted to the province from the present fiscal policy of the Dominion; but, on the other hand, much benefit. Besides what applies to the consumer of home manufactured lines of goods in Prince Edward Island, affects equally the people of the other provinces; and instead of enhancing the price of goods, it is notorious that since the adoption of the present fiscal policy, of which Messrs. Sullivan and Ferguson approve, the prices of many articles of consumption have declined in every part of Canada.

Messrs. Sullivan and Ferguson admit in a subsequent paragraph that the Island has prospered, as they put it, "notwithstanding the inaction of the Dominion Government." This statement, in view of what has already been stated, may be left to take care of itself; but the object of their representation appears to be to secure the laying of a metallic subway across the Straits of Northumberland, through which railway communication could be effected, "the cost of which undertaking," Messrs. Sullivan and Ferguson say, "would not exceed a sum which would not be unreasonable to ask the Government of Canada to expend." If it can be shown that such a work is practicable, that it can be constructed for a reasonable outlay, and maintained without a large expenditure, the matter seems to be one that may fairly be placed before the Canadian Government for consideration.

Messrs. Sullivan and Ferguson again return to the charge of the revenue contributed to the Dominion. They take exception to the statement that the island has received liberal treatment from the Dominion, and repeat that it pays more to the Dominion annually than it receives, which is certainly open to argument, although it does not bear upon the question of the feasibility of "continuous steam service."

Messrs. McLelan and Campbell say "the 'Northern Light' was placed at Charlottetown as headquarters, her officers and crew are inhabitants of the island, and her unceasing and hazardous efforts to make communication in the severest weather cannot be unknown to the Island Government." The delegates remark upon this. "The Committee of Council seem to entertain the idea that the officers and crew of the 'Northern Light,' being island men, are consequently bold enthusiasts, and would be willing to incur great risk in the effort to maintain communication with the mainland." They then go on apparently to complain that the running of the ship was left to the discretion of the officer in charge, and that he was ordered not to incur any undue risks. That unceasing and hazardous efforts have been made is proved by the memorial from Prince Edward Island to Her Majesty, which states that "at times she ('Northern Light') has been ice-bound for periods varying from ten to twenty-four days, to the imminent danger of passengers and mails. Upon one occasion, four years ago, some of the passengers, among them women and children, were forced, after remaining on board several days, to leave her and walk a distance of many miles to the shore, when, night overtaking them, they received injuries from cold and exposure which resulted ultimately in the death of one of the party." This shows that the officers and crew have made hazardous efforts to keep up communication, and the necessity of discretion, and the avoidance of undue risks. It also proves the impossibility of continuous steam service which the island insists on. It must be remarked that it was the officers of the "Northern Light" who gave evidence to the effect "that no steamship can be built capable of keeping up continuous communication in mid-winter between the island and the mainland."

Messrs. Sullivan and Ferguson conclude their rejoinder by saying, "With regard to the claim for compensation by reason of the non-fulfilment of the terms of Confederation, the undersigned submit that a review of the facts adduced will conclusively show that the Island has suffered great loss, and is therefore entitled to indemnity." In the first place, it is incorrect to say that the Terms of Confederation have not been complied with. Only one of the "terms" has been brought forward as not having been carried out, and proof has been adduced that continuous steam service has been provided, so far as was practicable. Daily steam communication is not feasible, it being impossible, in the opinion of competent witnesses, to construct a steamship to fulfil such conditions. The period of interruption prior to confederation has been reduced by two-thirds, and instead of suffering any injury the island has, since 1873, made rapid advances in wealth and prosperity, which may fairly be attributable to the more advantageous position the island occupies as a member of the Union, to the efforts of the Dominion Government to aid in the development of its resources, and to the vastly improved communication with the mainland that has been provided.

The foregoing remarks upon Messrs. Sullivan and Ferguson's letter are not

10

so complete as they might be made, owing to the short time that the undersigned has been in possession of the views of those gentlemen.

CHARLES TUPPER.

9, Victoria Chambers, London, S. W.,
March 12th, 1886.

[COPY.]

DEAR MR. SULLIVAN:— COLONIAL OFFICE, 18th March, 1886.

I have just received three copies of the enclosed memorandum from the printer, and I send you two of them.

Yours very truly.
ROBERT G. W. HERBERT.

LONDON,
March 22nd, 1886.

MY LORD,

The undersigned have perused the memorandum submitted by Sir Charles Tupper, High Commissioner for Canada, in reply to the letter which they had the honor of addressing to your Lordship on the 1st March instant; and they desire to offer a few observations thereon.

They entirely agree with the High Commissioner that it would have been far better had the special question at issue been dealt with upon its merits; but they are unable to concur with him in saying that for "the departure from this sound principle the Dominion Government cannot be blamed." The High Commissioner endeavors to justify the Dominion Government by stating that the irrelevant controversy was started in the memorial to Her Majesty, by drawing attention to the treatment received by British Columbia in the rapid construction of the Canadian Pacific Railway, although the population of white people in that Province was comparatively small. That reference was answered by the Committee of the Privy Council of Canada in the following words: "In a strictly local view it is not unjust to say that expenditure shall in some measure be governed by receipts, present or prospective," and this statement was followed by an elaborate calculation purporting to show the contributions of British Columbia and Prince Edward Island respectively to the General Treasury.

The undersigned, although well aware of the irrelevancy of the matter, and of the impropriety of the principle laid down by Messrs. McLelan and Campbell that communication with Prince Edward Island should be considered as a local work, and that expenditure thereon should to any extent be governed by receipts, present or prospective, felt it to be their duty to remonstrate that the Dominion Government are laboring under a grave, and for Prince Edward Island, a most unfortunate misapprehension, in regard to the revenue received from the Province, and having done so, it is not necessary to make further allusion to that branch of the subject.

With respect to the Halifax Fishery Award, the High Commissioner seems to be under the impression that the undersigned are not aware that prior to the Island's joining the Confederation it had made arrangements with the United States in regard to the inshore fisheries, differing from those made by Canada. The undersigned are not without knowledge of the agreement then made, but their recollection of it differs somewhat from that of the High Commissioner. The understanding then arrived at was come to by Prince Edward Island in compliance with the urgent request of Her Majesty's Imperial Government, in anticipation of the Treaty of Washington's taking effect, and especially in order to avoid complications between Great Britain and the United States. That the arrangement did not cover the period referred to was owing to the fact that the Dominion of Canada failed to take such action as was necessary to give it effect. The refund about £5,000, to which in this connection the High Commissioner refers, was paid, not to Prince Edward Island, as is stated, but to individual Canadian merchants and fishermen. The grievance of Prince Edward Island regarding the distribution of the amount of the Halifax Fishery Award has not, however, any connection with the question of interprovincial communication, and the reference to it by the undersigned was only made as appertaining to the discussion of comparative contributions, raised by the Dominion Government. The undersigned shall, therefore, make no further allusion to it now, except to say that they do not agree with the High Commissioner that the position of the Island in the matter is precisely the same as that of Nova Scotia and New Brunswick.

Under the terms of Confederation, the Dominion Government undertook to provide "efficient steam service for the conveyance of mails and passengers, to be established and maintained between the Island and the mainland of the Dominion, winter and summer, thus placing the Island in continuous communication with the Intercolonial Railway and the railway system of the Dominion." The question is, have the Dominion Government performed this obligation? They are forced to admit that they have failed. But the High Commissioner answers that a "regular daily steam service is an impossibility," and that "proof has been adduced that continuous steam service has been provided as far as was practicable." The report of the Parliamentary Committee of 1883 is referred to as justifying these statements; but the undersigned feel impelled to remark that a perusal of that report has led them to a different conclusion. It is said that the Island Government, prior to Confederation, had accomplished no more than the Dominion Government have done since that time, but it is apparently forgotten that one of the chief inducements to enter the union was to secure continuous steam service. The High Commissioner states that no representation was made in this matter to the Dominion Government till 1881, although the steamer named the *Northern Light* was put on in 1876. That the people of Prince Edward Island endured this grievance without formal remonstrance from their Government, not only from 1876 to 1881, but from 1873 to 1881, is a proof that they have acted reasonably in giving the Dominion Government ample time to carry out their undertaking, and should not now be used as an argument against their claim. The High Commissioner takes exception to the statement that the *Northern Light* was not specially "designed" for the service, and refers to the

Address to the Governor General adopted by the Legislature of Prince Edward Island in 1881, wherein that vessel is alluded to as having been "constructed expressly for the work." Both these expressions are correct. The *Northern Light* was "designed" for a totally different service—namely, for navigating fixed and comparatively thin ice on the River St. Lawrence—and, after having been so "designed," she was purchased by the Dominion Government and "constructed" for the service she has been attempting to perform. This is confirmed by Messrs. McLelan and Campbell, for they say, "The Dominion Government, after a most careful and anxious inquiry, contracted with a Mr. Sewell, of Quebec, to complete a powerful steamer on a model specially designed for ice service." They do not say, nor does the High Commissioner, that she was specially designed for the work to which she has been devoted, but it is stated that she was *completed* for that service.

The High Commissioner seems to labor under the impression that he has discovered a discrepancy in the statements in regard to the average period the *Northern Light* is unavailable during the winter, as in the communication of the undersigned it is given as seventy days, in the Address to Her Majesty in 1885, sixty-four days, and in the Report of the Parliamentary Committee in 1883, forty-eight days. These statements, we have every reason to believe, are all correct, for the periods to which they apply. The average time, when the Parliamentary Committee reported in 1883, was forty-eight days, which increased in 1885 to sixty-four days, and in 1886 to seventy days. It is here worthy of remark that the steam service instead of improving is, year after year, becoming less efficient and continuous. Last winter the vessel was laid up ninety days.

With reference to the failure of the Dominion Government to make any provision for the conveyance of passengers, the High Commissioner explains by quoting from a letter of the late Minister of Marine, Mr. McLelan, that the *Northern Light* made regular trips this season until 27th January. Mr. McLelan states: "the delegates crossed by that route, and I believe they said it was the first time that they had ever been brought over—that is, they had, on all previous occasions, to work their passage." In the opinion of the undersigned this is the strongest confirmatory proof of the allegation that "no sufficient disposition has been shown by the Dominion Government to fulfil their obligations towards the Island in this matter." Your Lordship will probably learn with surprise that for thirteen years the Government of Canada, notwithstanding their obligation to provide efficient steam communication for mails and passengers winter and summer, have allowed such a state of things to exist, and that a merit is now being made out of the circumstance that once, and that less than two months ago, in those thirteen years, even the official representatives of the Island Government were relieved of the labor of "working their passage." This favor will be still better appreciated when it is known that the delegates were only conveyed after a persistent remonstrance on their part against working their passage. All the other travellers, numbering about a dozen, were obliged to assist in drawing the boats.

It is said to be the contention of the Dominion Government that the utmost has been done to carry out the terms under which the Island entered the Union, that the efforts made by the *Northern Light* prove the imposibility of providing continuous steam service, and the report of the Parliamentary Committee is appealed to in verification of this contention. In that report it is recommended that the Government adopt Capes Traverse and Tormentine as the points of communication for mails and passengers, and the Committee also made several other recommendations which have not been acted upon by the Dominion Government, although three years have elapsed since that time. Beyond the abortive efforts of the *Northern Light* no attempt has been made to provide steam service. At the narrowest place—between Capes Traverse and Tormentine—steam, in any way, has never been applied, and no means of crossing have been used, except the ice-boat system, adopted about sixty years ago and continued, almost without improvement, to the present time. The Dominion Government, not having tried steam at the Capes, as recommended by the Parliamentary Committee, are in no better position now to say that steam communication is impracticable than they were at the time of Confederation.

The undersigned therefore submit that the Dominion Government have failed to carry out the terms of Confederation, and they are unable to agree with the High Commissioner that it is not a failure because the default is at present applied to only a part of those terms. When it is shown that the Dominion Government have failed in performing any portion of the conditions, it cannot surely be inconsistent with the fact to assert that there is a failure in carrying out the terms.

If what the Dominion Government have agreed to perform is impracticable by steam navigation, then it is clearly their duty to provide communication by other means, and should they ultimately fail and thus demonstrate the impossibility of their undertaking, then Prince Edward Island is unquestionably, on every principle of justice, entitled to an indemnity, covering the failure of the past and applying to the future, as the Province has performed its part of the compact and Canada receives, at least, its full consideration.

The contention of the High Commissioner that the progress of Prince Edward Island, referred to by the undersigned in their letter of 1st inst., "does not indicate that much injury has resulted to the Island from the want of continuous steam service, and clearly proves the benefit derived from the connection of the Island with the Confederation, and the improved service since 1873," is, the undersigned submit, wholly unwarranted. It is notorious that the progress of Prince Edward Island was equally great during the thirteen years previous to Confederation, when, the High Commissioner contends, the means of communication were less efficient than they have been since. The undersigned are not now called upon to express any opinion on the advantage or disadvantage of Confederation to Prince Edward Island, as that point is beside the question at issue.

The undersigned regret that they have been obliged to extend these observations further than they could desire, and they feel that after the lengthened interviews with which your Lordship has favored them, it is unnecessary to add to the information now in the Colonial Office, although the subject is by no means exhausted.

Prince Edward Island appeals to the Imperial Government, at whose request it entered the Union, to interpose their influence with the Government of Canada, in order that justice may be done in the premises, and that the harmony which is so desirable between the different members of the Confederation shall prevail.

In conclusion, the undersigned desire to express their sense of the deep obligation they are under to your Lordship for the courtesy that has been shown them, and for the readiness and attention with which all their communications have been received.

We have the honor to be,

Your Lordship's most obedient humble Servants,

W. W. SULLIVAN.

D. FERGUSON.

The Right Honorable Earl Granville, K. G.,
Secretary of State for the Colonies.

---

143 G. [COPY.]

Canada, No. 75.

Earl Granville to the Marquis of Lansdowne.

DOWNING STREET, 30th March, 1886.

MY LORD,—I duly received Your Lordship's despatch of the 19th of November last, enclosing an approved report of a Committee of the Privy Council for Canada, forwarding with other papers a joint address to the Queen from the Legislative Council and House of Assembly of Prince Edward Island. This address prays that Her Majesty will require that justice be done by the Government of Canada to Her Majesty's loyal subjects of that Province by the immediate establishment and "maintenance of efficient steam service, for the conveyance of mails and passengers between this Island and the Mainland of the Dominion, both winter and summer, so as to place the Island in continuous communication with the Intercolonial Railway, and the railway system of the Dominion;" and further that Her Majesty would be pleased to require that the Government of Canada should compensate the Island for the loss which, it is alleged, has resulted to its inhabitants, by reason of the non-fulfilment of the terms of Confederation in the particulars complained of in the address.

I also received your Despatch of the 30th January, with a further report of a committee of the Privy Council, on the subject of the Delegation appointed to support the prayer of the address.

Since the receipt of these papers, I have had the pleasure of receiving Mr.

Sullivan, the Premier and Attorney General, and Mr. Ferguson, the Provincial Secretary of Prince Edward Island, who had been appointed as Delegates to Her Majesty's Government, and on the 24th of last month they attended here by appointment, and favored me with a general statement of the circumstances under which the Legislatature of Prince Edward Island had addressed the Queen. I explained to them that the Queen had no power either by statute or otherwise, under the constitution of Canada, to give any direction in the matter, and that therefore I should not be able to advise Her Majesty, (who had been pleased to receive the address very graciously) to take any action upon it, but that it would give me much satisfaction, if by the exercise of any friendly offices which I could tender, I should be able to contribute to the settlement of a question in which the Provincial Government were so much interested. I added that I had confidence in the friendly spirit in which the matter at issue would be dealt with on both sides, and this led me to hope that some acceptable arrangement might be come to. I then gave the delegates a copy of the report of the Privy Council of Canada, dated the 7th of November last, which they had not previously received, and I informed them that after receiving and considering the observations which they might desire to make upon that report, I should be happy to see them again, and if it should be agreeable to both parties, to invite Sir Charles Tupper to be present on behalf of the Dominion Government at the interview.

On the 4th inst., I received from the Delegates the statement of which a copy is enclosed, and I communicated a copy of it to Sir Charles Tupper, who favoured me with his comments thereupon in a memorandum, of which a copy is also enclosed.

After perusing these papers I invited the Delegates and Sir Charles Tupper to meet me at this office on the 12th inst. The Delegates urged at length the claims and contentions of the Province, and laid before me the plans of a submarine line of communication which they understood to be feasible. Sir Charles Tupper then justified and explained the action of the Dominion Government adding personally and not speaking under instructions, that if it could be shown that the scheme of a "metallic subway" is really feasible at a moderate cost the Dominion Government would, no doubt, be ready to give their serious consideration to such a scheme.

As I stated in the earlier part of this despatch, although Her Majesty's Government is unable to take the question out of the hands of the Dominion Government, and although I have not seen more than a *prima facie* opinion as to the feasibility, at a moderate cost, of the proposal for its solution, I hope that it will be found to admit of a satisfactory settlement. On the one hand the expectations of the Province in regard to the establishment of a constant and efficient communication with the mainland have not been fulfilled, but on the other hand, the Dominion Government has shown that it has made considerable efforts to improve the communication in the face of serious physical difficulties during the winter season. There seems to be reason for doubting whether any really satisfactory communication by steamship can be regularly maintained all the year round, which makes it all the more important that the proposed "metallic subway" should receive a full, and if feasible, favourable consideration on the part of the Government of the Dominion.

The establishment of constant and speedy communication by rail would be a great advantage both to the Province and to the Dominion, and I should suppose that the development of the traffic on the Island railroads, and of the capabilities of the Province generally, would produce a large direct and indirect return on the expenditure.

It would reflect great credit on the Dominion Government, if, after connecting British Columbia with the Eastern Provinces by the Canadian Pacific Railway, it should now be able to complete its system of railway communication by an extension to Prince Edward Island.

I have, &c.,

(Signed) GRANVILLE.

No. 4471
on
No. 2014.

[COPY.]

SIR:—

OTTAWA, 17th April, 1886.

I have the honor to transmit to you herewith for the information of your Government copy of a Despatch to His Excellency the Governor General from the Right Honorable the Secretary of State for the Colonies with its enclosures, having reference to the Joint Address to the Queen from the Legislative Council and House of Assembly of Prince Edward Island on the subject of Communication between the Island and the Mainland, and referring to the recent visit to England of a Delegation from your Government in support of the prayer of the said Address.

I have the honor to be,

Sir,

Your Obedient Servant,

(Signed) J. A. CHAPLEAU,
Secretary of State.

His Honor
The Lieutenant Governor of
Prince Edward Island, Charlottetown.

www.ingramcontent.com/pod-product-compliance
Lightning Source LLC
Chambersburg PA
CBHW020239090426
42735CB00010B/1764
9783337175405